Contextualising Eating Disorders

This book rethinks the diagnosis and treatment of eating disorders by putting the spotlight on their social and societal contexts, examining how these behaviours are shaped by the difficult life conditions of those suffering.

Drawing on the lived experiences of nine women, this book uses in-depth case studies and interviews to discuss eating disorders with a Social Contextual Analysis framework. It prioritises the women's own voices about their life conditions and recovery to explore the behaviour of unusual eating patterns. The book identifies common social properties across the nine women, which will become essential context when considering treatment and therapy for unusual eating. Through this more compassionate approach, readers are presented with a detailed example of new ways to analyse and treat the behaviours of mental health and therapy outside of a DSM diagnosis.

Contextualising Eating Disorders is unique in its focus on giving priority to women's voices and the social contexts behind unusual eating and will be highly relevant for all professionals working with those with unusual eating patterns, as well as students and academics in the fields of social psychology and mental health. This book will also benefit those who themselves are suffering from unusual eating patterns they might not understand.

Bernard Guerin is Professor of Psychology at the University of South Australia. His research and writing try to integrate what we know from the social sciences to provide a contextual view of all human behaviour, talking and thinking.

Millie Tait is a Psychology Honours Graduate from the University of South Australia working in community services. She is interested in supporting people through their life situations labelled as 'mental health problems' without pathologising.

Scarlett Kraehe is a Bachelor of Psychology (Honours) Graduate from the University of South Australia with an interest in gender and race theory.

Nikia Bailey is a Psychologist holding a Master of Psychology (Clinical) from the University of South Australia.

Exploring the environmental and social foundations of human behaviour

Series Editor
Bernard Guerin
Professor of Psychology, University of South Australia

Can you imagine that everything people do, say and think is shaped directly by engaging with our many environmental and social contexts? Humans would then really be part of their environment.

For current psychology, however, people only engage with metaphorical 'internal' environments or brains events, and everything we do somehow originates hidden in there. But what if all that we do and think originated out in our worlds, and what we call 'internal' is merely language and conversations which were also shaped by engaging in our external discursive, cultural and societal environments?

Exploring the environmental and social foundations of human behaviour is an exciting new book series about developing the next generation of ways to understand what people do, say and think. Human behaviour is shaped through directly engaging in our diverse contexts of resources, social relationships, economics, culture, discourses, colonization, patriarchy, society, and the opportunities afforded by our birth contexts. Even language and thinking arise from our external social and discursive contexts, and so the 'internal' and brain metaphors will disappear as psychology becomes merged with the social sciences.

The series is therefore a-disciplinary and presents analyses or contextually-engaged research on topics which describe or demonstrate how human behaviour arises from direct engagement with the worlds in which we are embedded.

Find out more about this series here: www.routledge.com/Exploring-the-Environmental-and-Social-Foundations-of-Human-Behaviour/book-series/EESF

In this series:

Contextualising Eating Disorders

The Hidden Social Contexts of Unusual Eating

Bernard Guerin, Millie Tait, Scarlett Kraehe and Nikia Bailey

Routledge
Taylor & Francis Group

LONDON AND NEW YORK

Cover Image: Shutterstock © miniartkur

First published 2024
by Routledge
4 Park Square, Milton Park, Abingdon, Oxon OX14 4RN

and by Routledge
605 Third Avenue, New York, NY 10158

Routledge is an imprint of the Taylor & Francis Group, an informa business

British Library Cataloguing-in-Publication Data
A catalogue record for this book is available from the British Library

Library of Congress Cataloging-in-Publication Data
Names: Guerin, Bernard, 1957– author.
Title: Contextualising eating disorders : the hidden social contexts of
  unusual eating / Bernard Guerin, Millie Tait, Scarlett Kraehe and
  Nikia Bailey.
Description: Abingdon, Oxon ; New York, NY : Routledge, 2024. |
  Series: Exploring the environmental and social foundations of human
  behaviour | Includes bibliographical references and index.
Identifiers: LCCN 2023059181 (print) | LCCN 2023059182 (ebook) |
  ISBN 9781032592688 (hbk) | ISBN 9781032592657 (pbk) |
  ISBN 9781003453918 (ebk)
Subjects: LCSH: Eating disorders—Social aspects.
Classification: LCC RC552.E18 G84 2024 (print) | LCC RC552.E18
  (ebook) | DDC 616.85/26—dc23/eng/20240313
LC record available at https://lccn.loc.gov/2023059181
LC ebook record available at https://lccn.loc.gov/2023059182

ISBN: 978-1-032-59268-8 (hbk)
ISBN: 978-1-032-59265-7 (pbk)
ISBN: 978-1-003-45391-8 (ebk)

DOI: 10.4324/9781003453918

Typeset in Bembo
by Apex CoVantage, LLC

Contents

Figures

Tables

Preface

This book started as three Honours Research Theses. In 2020, Millie did her contextual research with three women who had 'recovered' from so-called eating disorders, supervised by Bernard Guerin. (The research processes are described in Chapter 4.) In 2021, two new Honours students, Scarlett and Nikia, were really interested in what Millie had found out so they also did contextual research with three women each who had recovered from so-called eating disorders.

We later hit on the idea of combining these into a book form, so the detailed life stories told by these nine women could be seen side-by-side. We have never seen an example before of Honours research being made into a book, but the research by all three was perfectly conducted and the results extremely interesting. So, we have done a book.

Contextual research is different to most research in psychology and is closer to social anthropology. This means that participants are not asked a standard set of questions but are allowed to talk freely and lead the conversations (informal conversations done several times rather than single interviews). This means that the research differed depending upon the women's stories to the researcher. So, all nine women in this research had very different conversations covering somewhat different points. For example, by 2021 we knew that language (and thinking) was important, so more themes were pursued along these lines.

Within all that diversity of life there were clear patterns in what had shaped these behaviours, and what had led to recovery, even though the details varied from woman to woman. Part of how we have structured this book is about keeping the diversity there for the reader while also showing the similar patterns. We move from full diversity (Chapters 5–13, the stories) to more (Chapter 14) and more (Chapter 15) of the similar patterns that can be seen, and which should direct any future interventions.

Who are the audiences for this book?

Our aim was not to produce a standard academic book, with research and statistics. We had three main audiences in mind in addition to academics.

First: for those who have had or still have these behaviours, currently labelled as 'eating disorders', who are probably not sure why they are doing these behaviours, let alone how to change them. We hope that the stories and the general pathways will be useful and interesting. None will have exact matches to these nine women, but some may find general patterns similar in their life and some ideas on how to change these, if they have not already done so in their own way.

Second: for those who work alongside people with these behaviours, to try and get them to see beyond the diagnoses and find out more about the broader contextual worlds of the people they converse with. These might be professionals or family; they might be psychiatrists or therapists; or they might be carers and nurses. We hope you can begin to see the wider picture going on here, led by our nine participants.

Third: for those who are affected by the mental health systems or who are working in those systems who no longer believe the psychiatric medical models or the clinical 'cognitive processing' models that pretend to explain what is going on (Chapter 2). Many have been impressed with the Power Threat Meaning Framework as an alternative, for example, or other sociological or 'eclectic' models.

The problem we find with most of these alternative models is: What do we do next? We can get rid of the DSM and biological models of mental health, but what can we do differently now? Where do we go from here? The people are still suffering, so where do we go from here?

We hope our book will show some paths forward in this—much more concrete patterns of what needs to be done next to replace the medical models and the DSM and diagnostics as the sole focus when trying to help people who find themselves with these unusual behaviours. In this book there are new ways of talking to people, and new ways of analysing what they tell you. Most diagnosis starts with talking about a person's life, or the basic demographics, but stops as soon as a suitable diagnosis is found. We show in this book that you can get *so much more* if you systematically let the person talk about all their life contexts, not just those relevant to getting a diagnosis.

We sincerely hope that all three audiences, and the usual academic suspects, can learn something from this book, whether about the behaviours labelled currently as 'eating disorders', or the methods by which you can talk to people (listen more than talk, actually) and learn from them *what has happened to them* to shape these scary and unwanted behaviours.

It is in this spirit that we have written this book. Enjoy, explore, learn and apply.

Acknowledgments

We all wish to sincerely thank the nine women who gave their time and their stories for our research. Although they have had their names changed and some identifying details disguised, their lives make up this book. We are ever grateful to them. In return, we have tried not to simplify and reduce their stories to the same thing. We have found ways to include the unique features of each of them while still providing the diversity of stories and lives they presented to us. Too often research squashes people's lives into the same pattern for everyone. Thank you one and all of the nine.

1 Introduction

I had these expectations from my parents to be a certain person, and I thought I was doing that right. But then I had peers then telling me because I was trying to do that, then I was—yeah so I was in this kind of vice, it was a really hard place to be in.

—Katrina

To this day, whenever I pick up a biscuit, I always remember my dad saying, 'Oh, you'll end up the size of a house'.

—Adora

I was always the one getting good grades and that just became the normal for me, so I stopped getting that praise. And what I did felt never good enough for my parents or my family. So I would just keep trying harder and harder. And I guess that manifested into my eating disorder. . . . I've always had to exercise more, eat less, look better, work harder.

—Fiona

Ideas around mental health have been changing over the last 20 or more years. For over a century the idea has been that a brain disease or a chemical imbalance in the brain led to the unusual looking behaviours that were called mental health issues. Closely following the mostly successful path in medicine, the strategy was to develop a categorisation of these diseases and then find specific treatments for each. Unfortunately, after decades, we are left with a weak categorisation system based only on an expert consensus, with only generic drugs and generic talking treatments.

Changing these ideas around mental health has come from many quarters, including psychology, social sciences, Indigenous elders, feminists and others (Boyle & Johnstone, 2020; Guerin, 2017, 2020). Diversity and differences exist within these new ideas, but the core of these proposed changes are the following:

- mental health is best viewed as a set of behaviours
- behaviours for our approach includes action, talking, thinking and feeling
- the behaviours of mental health do not *begin* or *originate* 'inside' a person
- a person's whole life is involved in shaping these behaviours

DOI: 10.4324/9781003453918-1

- the 'whole life' includes what are called spiritual, social, cultural and historical influences
- treatments need to change these life influences directly, rather than attempting to change life situations by only talking with a stranger, or altering brain chemistry

Many have written about the theoretical models regarding these whole life influences on the actions, talking, thinking and feelings that get labelled as 'mental health' symptoms. But we have not found many or any concerted attempts to demonstrate or describe in detail these influences in specific cases.

This book is, as such, *a concerted attempt to show by example how adjusting to bad life situations can indeed shape the behaviours still called 'mental health'*. We explored through contextual research (Guerin et al., 2024) the life situations of nine women who had 'eating disorder' labels from the DSM categorisation of mental disorders, due to their practices of eating and body behaviours (American Psychiatric Association, 2013). Such behaviours include: overeating, undereating, exercising, self-induced vomiting and other rituals to reduce food intake.

This book is not going to tell you everything you might have already read about eating disorders. Instead, we are going to provide a new way of looking at the behaviours involved and then focus on extremely detailed stories of nine women who went through all of this. We will not focus on their labels but on the actual behaviours of those women as they happened in their lives.

We are also going to concentrate on how the contexts and *events in these women's lives* influenced or shaped their eating and exercising behaviours. From this we will try to locate the main problems that the nine women were adjusting to, and propose a more effective framework for treatment and prevention.

Plan of the book

There are three very unequal sections of this book, and they each require a different method of reading.

The first section is more academic and outlines the medical models of mental health and eating disorders followed by some of the newer alternative models. The model we focus on is Social Contextual Analysis because it is the broadest, and we believe, most concrete. The first section concludes with a chapter about the research methods we used to learn all the contexts from the nine women and the ethical measures in place. This first section can be read before starting the second or as you go along. We suggest reading one or two of the women's narratives and fill in gradually from this turgid first section.

The second section consists of nine long (but greatly reduced) narratives about the women, the life situations that shaped their behaviours and what changed when those behaviours disappeared. In these narratives, we have strived to keep as much context as possible to demonstrate complexity and diversity of eating disorders, leaving the theory to the introductory chapters and summary chapters.

The third section has two summary chapters. Chapter 14 tries to summarise what we learned from the nine women's narratives while still respecting the diversity, contradictions and exceptions. The women had some similar patterns in their lives, but mostly they had very different stories to tell. Chapter 15 goes back to the Social Contextual model and summarises more succinctly the shared contexts that can produce the behaviours labelled as 'eating disorders'. We anticipate this model summary would show different patterns for research on different DSM categories, as the shaping of behaviours is unlikely to be completely random.

Chapter 15 also draws out implications for *treatment* (Guerin, 2022). If the behaviours of mental health originate in a person's life contexts and bad events they are trying to adjust to (which our research indicates is the case for eating disorders), then our treatments must be focused on *how we can change that person's life contexts—their life situations*. As you will see in Chapter 14, the eating disorder issues improved when the nine women left their bad life situations—mostly from events outside of any treatment—they got a job elsewhere, moved in with a boyfriend, etc.

These are nine real lives. To communicate as many details as possible that went into the development of eating disorders, there was a need to be matter of fact and focus on some of the saddest events. We acknowledge that this research cannot represent the complexity of the women's lived experiences and how they suffered and thrived in many ways, but we hope you can begin to see how the behaviours of mental health originate in a person's world as adaptation to bad circumstances, not from some independent agent hidden inside them.

References

American Psychiatric Association. (2013). *Diagnostic and statistical manual of mental disorders: DSM-5*. American Psychiatric Association.

Boyle, M., & Johnstone, L. (2020). *A straight talking introduction to the Power Meaning Threat Framework: An alternative to psychiatric diagnosis*. PCCS Books.

Guerin, B. (2017). *How to rethink mental illness: The human contexts behind the labels*. Routledge.

Guerin, B. (2020). *Turning mental health into social action*. Routledge.

Guerin, B. (2022). *Reimagining therapy through Social Contextual Analyses: Finding new ways to support people in distress*. Routledge.

Guerin, B., Thain, E., Stevens, K., Richards, A., & Leugi, G. B. (2024). *Doing contextual research: New ways to understand and influence yourself and other people*. Routledge.

Part 1

Background to the eating disorders behaviours

2 What the mainstream models say is happening with behaviours and recovery

In this chapter we will look at the mainstream approach to mental health and the attempt to *explain* eating disorder behaviours through a medical or diagnostic framework. Our research methodology (Chapter 4) was guided by critiques of the mainstream model which demonstrate its missing contextual detail. Behaviour is shaped by the life contexts of the people, and this has not really been studied.

What actually are eating disorder behaviours? Our starting points

Before looking at the various approaches, we should be clear about the behaviours involved in the diagnoses of eating disorders, whether or not they are considered an internal disorder or shaped by bad life events. Box 2.1 sets out the behaviours under consideration. While the DSM is clear about these behaviours, such behaviours are commonly shared by people *not* presenting with an eating disorder; therefore, observing these behaviours without any context tells us nothing. Clearly greater context is required, a gap our research seeks to fill.

What we already know is that these behaviours, presenting as a group of problem behaviours or as extreme behaviours, occur mainly with *young women*, especially in western developed countries (not in a lot of Asia until recently; Pike & Dunne, 2015). We need to find out what life contexts shape these as a group of behaviours, and why these behaviours in particular occur in *extreme forms* for some people but not others.

Mainstream views of eating disorders

In clinical psychology and psychiatry, eating disorders are dealt with by diagnosis and generic 'treatments'. We will introduce some of the problems with this diagnostic approach, and the lack of specific treatments for the diagnoses which is unlike diagnosis and treatment in physiological medicine.

DOI: 10.4324/9781003453918-3

Box 2.1 Common eating disorder behaviours from DSM-5 and elsewhere

The following are the behaviours from the DSM and elsewhere that we are investigating, divided into three groups for our purposes. Body-image concerns and fears of weight-gain have been found to be central within eating disorder psychopathology, suggesting that *language behaviours* may be core features in eating disorder psychopathology. For this reason we will single them out when discussing other approaches.

Food-related actions

- restriction of food (portions, fasting, avoiding specific foods)
- eating when not physically hungry, eating more rapidly than normal, eating until feeling uncomfortably full, eating alone to avoid others monitoring how much one is eating
- self-induced vomiting

Other actions

- persistent behaviour that interferes with weight-gain (excessive exercise, self-induced bowel movements, medication and stimulants)
- excessive observing of one's own body and others' bodies

Uses of language (including both talking and thinking)

- self-evaluation is unduly influenced by body shape and weight (i.e., excessive talking and thinking about one's own body and others' bodies).

Diagnosis

In clinical psychology and psychiatry, eating disorders are classified using the Diagnostic and Statistical Manual of Mental Disorders (DSM-5), which lists nine diagnostic categories (American Psychiatric Association, 2013). The most researched categories are *anorexia nervosa*, *bulimia nervosa* and more recently *binge eating disorder*, which are differentiated by their primary eating behaviours: restricting, compensating and gorging, respectively (Hay, 2020).

A commonly accepted problem with the DSM-5 is that it does not represent the true diversity and variability across eating disorders. Most instances fall under the category *unspecified*, which arose as a catch-all for those who do not meet the full criteria for one or multiple criteria (Galmiche et al., 2019; Mustelin et al., 2016). Additionally, people diagnosed with eating disorders are known to change their eating strategies over time (Allen et al., 2013; Castellini et al., 2011), but this is little understood.

Explanations and critique

The social context of eating disorders is supposedly captured within 'bio-psycho-social' models, but contextual importance is lost when the model is interpreted using the underlying assumption of a pathological complexity in psychiatry and clinical psychology, rather than life context complexity as will be described later (Culbert et al., 2015). A common interpretation is that individuals are *biologically predisposed* to develop *psychological traits* that make them *vulnerable* to *social stress* (Culbert et al., 2015). But this is both abstract and tautological, as highlighted by italicised words, which are not directly observable or are only observed as correlations ("*associated with*"). For example, eating disorders are *associated with* social experiences such as family dynamics, parenting styles, athlete groups, victimisation, bullying, abuse and trauma; however, it is also then suggested that "dysfunctional emotion regulation" and "maladaptive thoughts" *explain* the association (Brewerton, 2019; Caslini et al., 2016; Chami et al., 2019; Lie et al., 2019; Luca et al., 2016; Monteleone et al., 2020; Trottier & MacDonald, 2017; Stoyel et al., 2020).

Some have argued that one-directional interpretations of the bio-psycho-social model reduce people's social worlds to triggers of individual deficits, which become the undue focus of eating disorder research and treatment (Levine & Smolak, 2014). Psychologists have proposed ways to emphasise the social shaping of these individual traits like *emotion-regulation*, *perfectionism* and *self-esteem*. These approaches show how social relationships might shape these abstract individual traits, but they still assume that the verbal reports of these traits are valid observations of an inner state and a causal agent of distress. Even life history interviews conducted by Patching and Lawler (2009) report that eating disorder development could be attributed to a *perceived* lack of control, a *sense of* non-connectedness to family and peers.

The first problem with the research is that they rely on abstract concepts that are not much help since they cannot be observed. However, we can build on this if we treat 'true' reports of internal states as language behaviour learnt from society, groups and interpersonal relationships.

The second problem is that the factors are all correlational, which does not help us much, especially when they are verbal report measures of internal factors or states. Suggesting that if we change the way participants report their internal thoughts then we can change the eating disorder is a loose assumption at best. Such reasoning is the fallacy of cause and correlation. The only really observable correlates given earlier were dieting and overeating. But it does not really help us knowing that dieting and overeating are associated with eating disorders since those behaviours are how eating disorders are defined—this is tautological.

A third problem is that these abstract concepts and correlations tell us little about why this occurs for some young women. Many young women have these correlates (reports of low self-esteem, conflictual internal relationships, etc.) but do *not* have eating disorders.

Mainstream views of treatment

Despite diagnostic categories for eating disorder, the treatments are largely transdiagnostic Cognitive Behavioural Therapy, which is standard therapy and counselling, i.e., talking (Hay, 2020). The cognitive approach to treating eating disorders tends to assign a pre-existing template of cause and effect, leading to generic treatment options. CBT-E is a supposedly *enhanced* type of therapy for eating disorders because it talks about common pathologies found across eating disorders, derived from correlations: *self-esteem deficits, perfectionism, preoccupation with weight and shape*, and *interpersonal issues* (Murphy et al., 2010). But outcome rates for CBT-E rarely exceed 50%, dropout and relapse is common, and treatment only reaches around 30% of people with eating disorders (Atwood & Friedman, 2020). Despite facing real possibilities of *death*, those who have eating disorders cannot just 'will' it away with talking or thinking. Whatever language occurs for the person and in therapy, the words alone do not help reduce eating disorder behaviours. We need to look closer at how language is being used *in these people's worlds* rather than the words themselves.

Although current mainstream treatments might offer some support and results, there appears to be a gap in knowing what is really happening (Hay, 2020). Research shows that treatment effects for eating disorders are not long-lasting, and even after individuals no longer meet the diagnostic criteria, weight and body concerns often remain (Troscianko & Leon, 2020). Relapse following diagnosis and treatment is high; Grilo et al. (2012) found that 43% of participants relapsed at some point after recovery and stressful life events were a major predictor. But this research is done through a diagnostic framework that views successful treatment as something like a cure, and any remaining or returning behaviours indicate a disorder.

However, when people with lived experience of eating disorders define recovery, they put greater emphasis on social-emotional functioning rather than a complete remission of symptoms (Emanuelli et al., 2012; Slof-Op't Landt et al., 2019). Research also suggests that feedback from participants from inpatient and outpatient programmes for eating disorders indicate that treatment could be improved by increased focus on broader life and long-term issues (Churruca et al., 2019; Mitrofan et al., 2019). This all points to problems in the way eating disorders are understood and that treatments could be improved by investigating alternative models which aim to de-pathologise mental health symptoms.

There are many more criticisms of the medical models of mental health behaviours that cannot be presented here (Caplan, 1995; Davies, 2014; Guerin, 2017, 2020; Johnstone et al., 2018; Kinderman, 2019; Watson, 2019), but you can see enough of a problem with the abstract explanations, the over-interpretation of correlations and generic treatments that prevent exploration of the contextual life details so important to shaping behaviour.

Research outside psychiatry and psychology going beyond the medical models

Within a broader range of research, outside of psychiatry and clinical psychology, some clues can be found to help us understand the puzzle of eating disorders behaviours. These clues are still mostly abstract concepts based on the internal medical models that rely on correlations, but they can help us look for particulars in more concrete research.

We will present this broad research using a recent framework for detailing life contexts (Guerin, 2023), and organise these clues into four contextual forces that shape behaviour: societal, group or cultural, interpersonal and language. By considering the ways that contextual shaping is filtered through different levels of life: societal, group, interpersonal and language, we avoid accidentally creating simplistic context factors like gender, socio-economic status, etc.

Societal forces shaping behaviour

We are all shaped by vast societal forces, including economics, bureaucracy, patriarchy, colonisation, norms and the like, and we know from sociology that these are difficult to observe. Most people are not aware of societal forces shaping their behaviour, and even if they do know or feel it, they are still often not able to verbalise how.

Societal *discourses* are taken-for-granted ways of talking about life, which produce divisions of power because they privilege some people over others. A clue to observing societal discourse is when ideas seem to come from 'everyone' or a 'generalised other' rather than a specific audience or person, and this is why thoughts can seem like they are the *cause* of behaviour. We will see that these societal discourses play a large role in shaping the anxiety behaviours of eating disorders.

Although eating disorders impact a range of people, societal driven divisions indicate that the development of eating disorders predominantly occurs in *adolescence* and for *women* in *western cultures* (Galmiche et al., 2019; Hoek, 2016). Some researchers present eating disorders as solutions to the dilemmas of powerlessness and oppression experienced by women (Maine, 2009). Sociologists and critical feminists study the negative power of patriarchy on women and negative power of capitalism on individuals (Malson & Burns, 2009; Schmitt, 2017). Although everyone who shares these contexts does not develop disordered eating, they are prevalent in eating disorders (Adler, 2013).

The impact of patriarchy and capitalism in shaping eating disorders is often reduced to media images of women's bodies, especially thin and sexualised bodies which accompany ideas that thinness is healthy, sexy and powerful (Baldwin, 2006; Derenne & Beresin, 2006; LaMarre & Rice, 2016; Papathomas et al., 2018; Rodgers & Melioli, 2016). While such research provides a clue as to one of the significant ways that societal discourses are disseminated, the effect of the media is often explained by *internalisation*, sometimes said to be an individual trait. From our contextual lens, *internalisation* really means that individuals learn to talk and therefore think about particular societal discourses.

Women's bodies and behaviours become sites of discourses, which can be restrictive if being a woman means being objectified, sexualised, disciplined and passive by the whole of society and not through anything you have done (Malson & Burns, 2009; Musolino et al., 2015; Piran, 2017). Societal changes driving increased *healthism* in recent years have even led to the proposal of a new eating disorder called orthorexia (Hanganu-Bresch, 2020). Contrary to accounts of *internalisation*, which is a passive response to discourse, some individuals with anorexia may be responding in defiance to dominant discourse (Halse et al., 2007). But discourses alone cannot *explain* eating disorders because they are shared by the larger population who are 'normal' and 'healthy' (LaMarre & Rice, 2016; Woolhouse et al., 2012).

Furthermore, studies have indicated that the increasing global prevalence of eating disorders, which was traditionally attributed to the spread of thin body ideals in western media, has been conflated with the rise of industrialisation and modernisation (Pike et al., 2014; Pike & Dunne, 2015). Research suggests these economic changes are altering relationships and introducing conflicting discourses of gender, marriage and adulthood, which are associated with women's eating disorders (Pike & Borovoy, 2004). This provides a strong indication that societal forces do shape eating disorders beyond the interpersonal or media ideals, to socio-cultural and political forces (Woolhouse & Day, 2015).

Group and other cultural forces shaping behaviour

Society contributes to shaping the behaviours of eating disorders largely through societal discourses, but people are also shaped by their smaller groups and cultural communities. One way that this may be done is through fitting in to important resource groups like family and friends.

Women who experienced praise from their family and friends for their weight-loss and punishment for their weight-gain are more likely to develop disordered eating behaviours (Gillison et al., 2016; Balantekin et al., 2014). Studies have observed that oftentimes, body-image ideals and eating disorder behaviours can develop and worsen within female friendship cliques, sometimes this is called 'social contagion' (Allison et al., 2014; Allison et al., 2021; Eisenberg & Neumark-Sztainer, 2010). But studies which talk to a diversity of women show how the renegotiation of discourses within groups makes those that accompany eating disorders and its effect on relationships unique, numerous and changing (Cheney et al., 2018; Darmon, 2009; Eli & Warin, 2018; Morris & Szabo, 2013; Moulding, 2016).

Eli and Warin (2018) argued that viewing mental health through an anthropological lens can provide important insights into what constitutes the culture of eating disorders. Eli and Warin (2018) and Musolino et al. (2020) observed that family relations, mass media, control, body-image, unfortunate life contexts and political contexts are important in the development and maintenance of eating disorders. Most of these factors draw on socio-cultural discourses in which body-image may be more accurately attributed to defects in society rather than individuals (Moulding & Hepworth, 2001).

The development of eating disorders is *associated* with bad life situations involving schools, homes and jobs; relationship changes, loss and bereavement; illness and abuse; bullying and problematic parent relationships (Berge et al., 2012; Castañeda et al., 2018; Goldschen et al., 2019; Patel et al., 2016; Reid et al., 2020). These closely resemble the sociological findings of early life contexts but are from smaller grouping within society.

Interpersonal forces shaping behaviour

Direct interpersonal interactions promote the group forces shaping eating dis-order behaviours. A few studies identify bereavement, negligence by caregiv-ers, strict and demanding relationships, and trauma as factors worth following up (Bekiaris & Koletsi, 2019; Patching & Lawler, 2009; Pettersen et al., 2013; Redenbach & Lawler, 2003; Stockford et al., 2019). Bad life situations seem to derive from interpersonal forces within families even though they originate in wider societal or group contexts. The generic interpersonal problems, unem-ployment, medical complications, depression, anxiety, substance-use problems and self-harm *associated* with eating disorders are also *potential consequences* of the contextual forces shaping bad life situations, rather than the bad life situations themselves. Both major alternatives to the medical models outlined later already incorporate these sorts of research findings from sociology and elsewhere, as major bad life events generated by society rather than the individuals involved.

Women's narratives of recovery have been found to involve verbal concepts around the self, such as acceptance, knowledge, esteem, connection and trans-formation (Dark & Carter, 2019; Patching & Lawler, 2009; Stockford et al., 2019; Wetzler, 2020). These are often treated as purely internal states, but the 'self' is a way of talking for others in society, groups or interpersonal relation-ships (Guerin, 2023). Most of our interpersonal interactions use language as the primary means (Guerin, 2023), and as would be expected, discourses main-tained by interpersonal interaction figure predominantly.

Turning points for recovery also often accompany realisations of how dis-ordered eating negatively interfered with contexts like jobs, education, rela-tionships and sport performance (Arthur-Cameselle & Curcio, 2018; Pettersen et al., 2013; Redenbach & Lawler, 2003). These directly relate to more concrete social resources including new interests and activities, jobs, setting boundaries, new relationships, changing priorities and counterculture communities (Dark & Carter, 2019; Matusek & Knudson, 2009). But the details of how these general themes occur in real lives are still needed.

Language forces and thinking

We have seen indications, albeit from correlational and somewhat abstract evi-dence, that discourse shapes aspects of eating disorder behaviours, and that these are promulgated through societal, group and interpersonal forces. Much of this discursive force is observable in the bits of language *not spoken out loud*, which in the research is referred to as *thinking, maladaptive thoughts, rumination, anxiety*, and *internalisation* (Rivière & Douilliez, 2017; Zaitsoff et al., 2002). Some research has suggested that *maladaptive thoughts* and *rumination* increase as eating disorders worsen and decrease as people begin to recover (Rawal et al., 2010). But we also saw in previous sections that many people share the same discourse and similar thoughts without having eating disorders.

Part of the problem here is that the medical and psychological models, as well as a lot of the social science models, still see thinking as an internal, personal activity not amenable to observation except by self-reporting. They also see it as an internal state that directly controls and shapes behaviour, but which is awkwardly difficult to handle because it is internal and cannot be directly changed except by changing a person's talking. We will come back to this later because it is important to consider where exactly these thoughts are originating and how they work. There is another model of mental health that has an alternative way of dealing with thinking, which allows it to be analysed and observed.

References

Adler, A. (2013). *The practice and theory of individual psychology* (Vol. 133). Routledge.

Allen, K., Byrne, S., Oddy, W., & Crosby, R. (2013). DSM—IV—TR and DSM-5 eating disorders in adolescents: Prevalence, stability, and psychosocial correlates in a population-based sample of male and female adolescents. *Journal of Abnormal Psychology, 122*(3), 720.

Allison, S., Warin, M., & Bastiampillai, T. (2014). Anorexia nervosa and social contagion: Clinical implications. *Australian & New Zealand Journal of Psychiatry, 48*(2), 116–120.

Allison, S., Warin, M., Bastiampillai, T., Looi, J. C., & Strand, M. (2021). Recovery from anorexia nervosa: The influence of women's sociocultural milieux. *Australasian Psychiatry, 3*(1).

American Psychiatric Association. (2013). *Diagnostic and statistical manual of mental disorders DSM-5.* American Psychiatric Association.

Arthur-Cameselle, J., & Curcio, M. (2018). Turning the corner: A comparison of collegiate athletes' and non-athletes' turning points in eating disorder recovery. *Journal of Clinical Sport Psychology, 12*(4), 595–613.

Atwood, M., & Friedman, A. (2020). A systematic review of enhanced cognitive behavioural therapy (CBT-E) for eating disorders. *International Journal of Eating Disorders, 53*(3), 311–330.

Balantekin, K. N., Savage, J. S., Marini, M. E., & Birch, L. L. (2014). Parental encouragement of dieting promotes daughters' early dieting. *Appetite, 80*(6), 190–196.

Baldwin, C. (2006). *How the media shape young women's perceptions of self-efficacy, social power and class: Marketing sexuality.* Edwin Mellen Press.

Bekiaris, D., & Koletsi, M. (2019). Subjective experience of positive emotions and impact of disordered eating behaviours in individuals with bulimia nervosa. *Dialogues in Clinical Neuroscience & Mental Health, 2*(1), 37–54.

Berge, J., Loth, K., Hanson, C., Croll-Lampert, J., & Neumark-Sztainer, D. (2012). Family life cycle transitions and the onset of eating disorders: A retrospective grounded theory approach. *Journal of Clinical Nursing, 21*(10), 1355–1363.

Brewerton, T. (2019). An overview of trauma-informed care and practice for eating disorders. *Journal of Aggression, Maltreatment & Trauma, 28*(4), 445–462.

Caplan, P. J. (1995). *They say you're crazy: How the world's most powerful psychiatrists decide who's normal.* Life Long.

Caslini, M., Bartoli, F., Crocamo, C., Dakanalis, A., Clerici, M., & Carrà, G. (2016). Disentangling the association between child abuse and eating disorders: A systematic review and meta-analysis. *Psychosomatic Medicine, 78*(1), 79–90.

Castañeda, L., Palos, P., Heredia, M., & Santoncini, C. (2018). Parents' and daughters' perception of family aspects associated with the onset of an eating disorder. *Revista Mexicana de Trastornos Alimentarios, 9*(1), 71–81.

Castellini, G., Sauro, C. L., Mannucci, E., Ravaldi, C., Rotella, C. M., Faravelli, C., & Ricca, V. (2011). Diagnostic crossover and outcome predictors in eating disorders according to DSM-IV and DSM-V proposed criteria: A 6-year follow-up study. *Psychosomatic Medicine, 73*(3), 270–279.

Chami, R., Monteleone, A., Treasure, J., & Monteleone, P. (2019). Stress hormones and eating disorders. *Molecular and Cellular Endocrinology, 497*, 110349.

Cheney, A., Sullivan, S., & Grubbs, K. (2018). The morality of disordered eating and recovery in southern Italy. *Medical Anthropology Quarterly, 32*(3), 443–457.

Churruca, K., Ussher, J., Perz, J., & Rapport, F. (2019). It's always about the eating disorder: Finding the person through recovery-oriented practice for bulimia. *Culture, Medicine, and Psychiatry*, 1–18.

Culbert, K., Racine, S., & Klump, K. (2015). Research review: What we have learned about the causes of eating disorders—a synthesis of sociocultural, psychological, and biological research. *Journal of Child Psychology and Psychiatry, 56*(11), 1141–1164. https://doi.org/10.1111/jcpp.12441.

Dark, E., & Carter, S. (2019). Shifting identities: Exploring occupational identity for those in recovery from an eating disorder. *Qualitative Research Journal, 20*(1), 127–139.

Darmon, M. (2009). The fifth element: Social class and the sociology of anorexia. *Sociology, 43*(4), 717–733.

Davies, J. (2014). *Cracked: Why psychiatry is doing more harm than good.* Icon Books.

Derenne, J. L., & Beresin, E. V. (2006). Body image, media, and eating disorders. *Academic Psychiatry, 30*(3), 257–261.

Eisenberg, M. E., & Neumark-Sztainer, D. (2010). Friends' dieting and disordered eating behaviours among adolescents five years later: Findings from Project EAT. *Journal of Adolescent Health, 47*(1), 67–73.

Eli, K., & Warin, M. (2018). Anthropological perspectives on eating disorders: Deciphering cultural logics. *Transcultural Psychiatry, 55*(4), 443–453.

Emanuelli, F., Waller, G., Jones-Chester, M., & Ostuzzi, R. (2012). Recovery from disordered eating: Sufferers' and clinicians' perspectives. *European Eating Disorders Review, 20*(5), 363–372.

Galmiche, M., Déchelotte, P., Lambert, G., & Tavolacci, M. P. (2019). Prevalence of eating disorders over the 2000–2018 period: A systematic literature review. *The American Journal of Clinical Nutrition, 109*(5), 1402–1413.

Gillison, F. B., Lorenc, A. B., Sleddens, E. F., Williams, S. L., & Atkinson, L. (2016). Can it be harmful for parents to talk to their child about their weight? A meta-analysis. *Preventive Medicine, 93*(1), 135–146,

Goldschen, L., Lundblad, W., Fertig, A., Auster, L., Schwarzbach, H., & Chang, J. (2019). Navigating the university transition among women who self-report an eating disorder: A qualitative study. *International Journal of Eating Disorders, 52*(7), 795–800.

Grilo, C. M., Pagano, M. E., Stout, R. L., Markowitz, J. C., Ansell, E. B., Pinto, A., Zanarini, M. C., Yen, S., & Skodol, A. E. (2012). Stressful life events predict eating disorder relapse following remission: Six-year prospective outcomes. *International Journal of Eating Disorders, 45*(2), 185–192.

Guerin, B. (2017). *How to rethink mental illness: The human contexts behind the labels.* Routledge.

Guerin, B. (2020). *Turning mental health into social action.* Routledge.

Guerin, B. (2022). *Reimagining therapy through Social Contextual Analyses: Finding new ways to support people in distress.* Routledge.

Guerin, B. (2023). *The four forces that shape human behaviour: A more exhaustive framework for the analysis and change of human behaviour.* Unpublished paper, University of South Australia.

Halse, C., Honey, A., & Boughtwood, D. (2007). The paradox of virtue: (Re) thinking deviance, anorexia and schooling. *Gender and Education, 19*(2), 219–235.

Hanganu-Bresch, C. (2020). Orthorexia: Eating right in the context of healthism. *Medical Humanities, 46*(3), 311–322.

Hay, P. (2020). Current approach to eating disorders: A clinical update. *Internal Medicine Journal, 50*(1), 24–29.

Hoek, H. (2016). Review of the worldwide epidemiology of eating disorders. *Current Opinion in Psychiatry, 29*(6), 336–339.

Johnstone, L., Boyle, M., Cromby, J., Dillon, J., Harper, D., Kinderman, P., . . . Read, J. (2018). *The power threat meaning framework: Towards the identification of patterns in emotional distress, unusual experiences and troubled or troubling behaviour, as an alternative to functional psychiatric diagnosis.* British Psychological Society.

Kinderman, P. (2019). *A manifesto for mental health: Why we need a revolution in mental health care.* Palgrave Macmillan.

LaMarre, A., & Rice, C. (2016). Normal eating is counter-cultural: Embodied experiences of eating disorder recovery. *Journal of Community & Applied Social Psychology, 26*(2), 136–149.

Levine, M., & Smolak, L. (2014). Paradigm clash in the field of eating disorders: A critical examination of the biopsychiatric model from a sociocultural perspective. *Advances in Eating Disorders: Theory, Research and Practice, 2*(2), 158–170.

Lie, S., Rø, Ø., & Bang, L. (2019). Is bullying and teasing associated with eating disorders? A systematic review and meta-analysis. *International Journal of Eating Disorders, 52*(5), 497–514.

Luca, C., Silvia, C., Giulia, B., & Renata, T. (2016). Do parental traumatic experiences have a role in the psychological functioning of early adolescents with binge eating disorder? *Eating and Weight Disorders-Studies on Anorexia, Bulimia and Obesity, 21*(4), 635–644.

Maine, M. (2009). Beyond the medical model: A feminist frame for eating disorders. In M. Maine, W. N. Davis, & J. Shure (Eds.), *Effective clinical practice in the treatment of eating disorders: The heart of the matter* (Vol. 3, Issue 17). Routledge/Taylor & Francis Group.

Malson, H., & Burns, M. (Eds.). (2009). *Critical feminist approaches to eating dis/orders.* Routledge.

Matusek, J., & Knudson, R. (2009). Rethinking recovery from eating disorders: Spiritual and political dimensions. *Qualitative Health Research, 19*(5), 697–707.

Mitrofan, O., Petkova, H., Janssens, A., Kelly, J., Edwards, E., Nicholls, D., Mcnicholas, F., Simic, M., Eisler, I., Ford, T., & Byford, S. (2019). Care experiences of young people with eating disorders and their parents: Qualitative study. *BJPsych Open, 5*(1).

Monteleone, A., Ruzzi, V., Patriciello, G., Pellegrino, F., Cascino, G., Castellini, G., Steardo, L., Monteleone, P., & Maj, M. (2020). Parental bonding, childhood maltreatment and eating disorder psychopathology: An investigation of their interactions. *Eating and Weight Disorders-Studies on Anorexia, Bulimia and Obesity, 25*(3), 577–589.

Morris, P., & Szabo, C. (2013). Meanings of thinness and dysfunctional eating in black South African females: A qualitative study. *African Journal of Psychiatry, 16*(5), 338–342.

Moulding, N. (2016). Gendered intersubjectivities in narratives of recovery from an eating disorder. *Affilia, 31*(1), 70–83.

Moulding, N., & Hepworth, J. (2001). Understanding body image disturbance in the promotion of mental health: A discourse analytic study. *Journal of Community & Applied Social Psychology, 11*(4), 305–317.

Murphy, R., Straebler, S., Cooper, Z., & Fairburn, C. (2010). Cognitive behavioural therapy for eating disorders. *The Psychiatric Clinics of North America*, *33*(3), 611–627.

Musolino, C. M., Warin, M., & Gilchrist, P. (2020). Embodiment as a paradigm for understanding and treating SE-AN: Locating the self in culture. *Frontiers in Psychiatry*, *11*(1), 534–541.

Musolino, C. M., Warin, M., Wade, T., & Gilchrist, P. (2015). 'Healthy anorexia': The complexity of care in disordered eating. *Social Science & Medicine*, *139*(1), 18–25.

Mustelin, L., Lehtokari, V., & Keski-Rahkonen, A. (2016). Other specified and unspecified feeding or eating disorders among women in the community. *International Journal of Eating Disorders*, *49*(11), 1010–1017.

Papathomas, A., White, H. J., & Plateau, C. R. (2018). Young people, social media, and disordered eating. In *Young people, social media and health* (pp. 101–117). Taylor & Francis.

Patching, J., & Lawler, J. (2009). Understanding women's experiences of developing an eating disorder and recovering: A life history approach. *Nursing Inquiry*, *16*(1), 10–21.

Patel, K., Tchanturia, K., & Harrison, A. (2016). An exploration of social functioning in young people with eating disorders: A qualitative study. *PLoS ONE*, *11*(7), e0159910.

Pettersen, G., Thune-Larsen, K., Wynn, R., & Rosenvinge, J. (2013). Eating disorders: Challenges in the later phases of the recovery process: A qualitative study of patients' experiences. *Scandinavian Journal of Caring Sciences*, *27*(1), 92–98.

Pike, K. M., & Borovoy, A. (2004). The rise of eating disorders in Japan: Issues of culture and limitations of the model of "westernisation". *Culture, Medicine and Psychiatry*, *28*(4), 493–531.

Pike, K. M., & Dunne, P. E. (2015). The rise of eating disorders in Asia: A review. *Journal of Eating Disorders*, *3*(33).

Pike, K. M., Hoek, H., & Dunne, P. E. (2014). Cultural trends and eating disorders. *Current Opinion in Psychiatry*, *27*(6), 436–442.

Piran, N. (2017). *Journeys of embodiment at the intersection of body and culture: The developmental theory of embodiment*. Academic Press.

Rawal, A., Park, R. J., & Williams, J. M. G. (2010). Rumination, experiential avoidance, and dysfunctional thinking in eating disorders. *Behaviour Research and Therapy*, *48*(9), 851–859.

Redenbach, J., & Lawler, J. (2003). Recovery from disordered eating: What life histories reveal. *Contemporary Nurse*, *15*(1–2), 148–156.

Reid, M., Wilson-Walsh, R., Cartwright, L., & Hammersley, R. (2020). Stuffing down feelings: Bereavement, anxiety and emotional detachment in the life stories of people with eating disorders. *Health and Social Care in the Community*, *28*, 979–987.

Rivière, J., & Douilliez, C. (2017). Perfectionism, rumination, and gender are related to symptoms of eating disorders: A moderated mediation model. *Personality and Individual Differences*, *116*(1), 63–68.

Rodgers, R. F., & Melioli, T. (2016). The relationship between body image concerns, eating disorders and internet use, part I: A review of empirical support. *Adolescent Research Review*, *1*(2), 95–119.

Schmitt, M. (2017). Dysfunctional capitalism: Mental illness, schizoanalysis and the epistemology of the negative in contemporary cultural studies. *Psychoanalysis, Culture & Society*, *22*(3), 298–316.

Slof-Op't Landt, M., Dingemans, A., de la Torre Y Rivas, J., & van Furth, E. (2019). Self-assessment of eating disorder recovery: Absence of eating disorder psychopathology is not essential. *International Journal of Eating Disorders*, *52*(8), 956–961.

Stockford, C., Stenfert Kroese, B., Beesley, A., & Leung, N. (2019). Women's recovery from anorexia nervosa: A systematic review and meta-synthesis of qualitative research. *Eating Disorders, 27*(4), 343–368.

Stoyel, H., Slee, A., Meyer, C., & Serpell, L. (2020). Systematic review of risk factors for eating psychopathology in athletes: A critique of an etiological model. *European Eating Disorders Review, 28*(1), 3–25.

Troscianko, E. T., & Leon, M. (2020). Treating eating: A dynamical systems model of eating disorders. *Frontiers in Psychology, 11*(1801), 55–64.

Trottier, K., & MacDonald, D (2017). Update on psychological trauma, other severe adverse experiences and eating disorders: State of the research and future research directions. *Current Psychiatry Reports, 19*(8), 45.

Watson, J. (2019). *Drop the disorder: Challenging the culture of psychiatric diagnosis.* PCCS Books.

Wetzler, S., Hackmann, C., Peryer, G., Clayman, K., Friedman, D., Saffran, K., Silver, J., Swarbrick, M., Magill, E., van Furth, E., & Pike, K. (2020). A framework to conceptualise personal recovery from eating disorders: A systematic review and qualitative meta-synthesis of perspectives from individuals with lived experience. *The International Journal of Eating Disorders, 53*(8), 1188–1203.

Woolhouse, M., & Day, K. (2015). *Food, eating, and 'eating disorders': Analysing adolescents' discourse.* In M. O'Reilly & J. N. Lester (Eds.), The Palgrave handbook of child mental health (p. 422–437). Palgrave Macmillan/Springer Nature.

Woolhouse, M., Day, K., Rickett, B., & Milnes, K. (2012). 'Cos girls aren't supposed to eat like pigs are they?' Young women negotiating gendered discursive constructions of food and eating. *Journal of Health Psychology, 17*(1), 46–56.

Zaitsoff, S. L., Geller, J., & Srikameswaran, S. (2002). Silencing the self and suppressed anger: Relationship to eating disorder symptoms in adolescent females. *European Eating Disorders Review: The Professional Journal of the Eating Disorders Association, 10*(1), 51–60.

3 What alternative models say is happening with unusual eating behaviours

The following chapter presents a brief introduction to some alternative models of mental health and introduces our thinking on the behaviours of eating disorders. We will explain what the alternatives to diagnostic models look like, and how this changes what we do in research. We will not elaborate on the shaping of eating disorders here as this is better covered through the nine women's stories. The proof of these approaches will be in those research results.

The two main alternatives currently are the Power Threat Meaning (PTM) Framework and Social Contextual Analysis (SCA), which have much in common and appeared around the same time (Boyle & Johnstone, 2020; Guerin, 2017, 2020, 2022; Johnstone et al., 2018). The basic Social Contextual Analysis of mental health behaviours is given in Box 3.1. The first parts overlap extensively with the Power Threat Meaning Framework's approach.

The PTM Framework was developed as an alternative to the diagnostic model of mental health, and the main application is to produce a narrative that can be used in therapy or case formulation. The PTM is a broad framework for understanding distress, and it is left purposely abstract to work alongside other current understandings including biological and cognitive models.

The approaches are not all new but are the most recently developed frameworks based upon an accumulation of many years of contextual research from a diversity of disciplines. The most important similarity is that they consider mental health symptoms to exist within the spectrum of normal behaviour, which is not *caused* by something inside but shaped by social experiences and societal contexts. Both alternatives consider the effects of power relations between people, but PTM emphasises the effect of negative power on core human needs, while SCA emphasises a person's inability to have an effect within their unique context because of bad situations which are not always obviously negative.

We will expand on SCA as the methods are better known (Guerin et al., 2024), and the aim of talking to the nine women in this research was to get as much contextual detail of their lives before, during and after they showed behaviours of eating disorders.

The basic idea is that behaviours of mental health are shaped by the life contexts in which people are trying to live, but there are specific conditions which

DOI: 10.4324/9781003453918-4

Box 3.1 Basic contextual model of behaviours labelled as 'mental health'

The following model of mental health demonstrates how these behaviours are social and neither mental nor about health.

1. Bad life situations →
Strong oppression or life restrictions
Many possible alternative normal behaviours are blocked
Living with oppression, bullying or violence
Living with poverty
Abuse of all sorts: physical, sexual, power, control
Other traumatic events of all sorts

2. These shape a lot of life responses →
Escape the bad life contexts
Fight or *physically resist* the bad life contexts
Talk their way out of the bad life contexts
Change the bad life contexts
Exit the bad life contexts
Distract themselves from the bad life contexts
'*Put up with*' the bad life contexts
Merely *survive* the bad life contexts
Hide the bad life contexts so at least other people do not make it worse; make things secret (which causes collateral effects)

3. These shape a lot of difficult and often damaging life patterns →
Crime, violence, bullying your way out, etc.
Escape or exiting the situations
Avoidance, drugs or distraction from your situation
'Putting up with it' hoping for a change
Talking your way out by conning, exploitation, etc.

4. But under three special life contexts the mental health behaviours are shaped→
When responses which might be expected in normal circumstances to help change the bad situations are not possible
When any alternative behaviours are blocked or restricted, usually by people or bureaucracies
When the sources of, or responsibility for, the bad life situations are not easy to observe

5. Then mental health behaviours are shaped →
Normal behaviours which become exaggerated or morphed when they have no effect to change things
Behaviours which might be unrelated to the immediate situation so they will not make sense to casual observers

Language and non-language behaviours shaped in different ways
Behaviours which can then become chronic if they get locked into the bad
  life situations

6. Which behaviours occur depends on circumstances and which behaviours are possible →
Behaviours which appear to give some control
Behaviours which are even possible given the life restrictions and
  oppressions
Behaviours already known by observation of others and media
Behaviours which have been modelled by others around or are salient
Behaviours which can be exaggerated and morphed if necessary
Behaviours requiring few resources

shape the large range of behaviours that can be considered 'disordered'. All of these properties give the behaviours of mental health their surreal qualities, and the idea that they have seemingly sprung out of nowhere (or seem to be a brain malfunction).

First. To start (from Box 3.1), the behaviours of mental health are found when the person has been living in bad life situations, whether chronic or short-term. As shown in Box 3.2, these situations are diverse.

Of particular interest for this book are the two bad life situations that are highlighted in italics in Box 3.2, situations which do not always occur with overtly bad or abusive means. People can live in households with loving families but have all their behaviours controlled and with limited options, and these are the kind of restrictive life contexts which our research participants spoke about.

Second. The next point is that bad life conditions do not shape *only* the behaviours of mental health, but many other strategies are shaped such as: escaping; fighting; bullying your way out; talking your way out; exiting the bad life situation; and distracting oneself from the situation (Box 3.1). In many cases these strategies do little harm and are short-lived and can be effective in changing a person's situation for the better. These strategies are likely tried by every person in a bad life situation, and the people with mental health problems have likely tried them but with no success.

Third. Not all these shaped strategies lead to the behaviours of mental health. The strong correlations between bad life situations and mental health are shared with criminality and other forms of deviance. But compared to mental health these other deviant behaviours require additional resources in order for them to be accessed and sustained. Not just anyone can take up crime, form a gang or join a cult. Likewise, even exiting a bad life situation or changing lifestyle (for example, moving to the country) requires resources, skills, money and social networks, limiting its availability to many people.

Box 3.2 Some bad life situations

Violence	Bullying over time, especially:
Crime	–in school, work, family
Long-term drug habits	Unemployment or bad jobs
Poverty	Death of close family or friends
Traumatic events of all sorts:	*Lack of opportunities, or silencing*
–long term or short term	*Strong restrictions imposed:*
Abuse of all sorts:	*–many behaviours become blocked*
–physical, sexual, power, control	Exclusion or discrimination:
Combat and fighting	–from social relationships
Oppression and violent control:	Having disabilities:
–taken by individuals or groups	–reduced behavioural repertoires
Forced displacement	Not fitting in to world born into
	Sometimes hospitalisation and medication

Fourth. It is often unclear why the bad situations are happening when the behaviours of mental health are shaped, meaning they are often attributed to the person themselves. If there is an understanding of why a bad situation is occurring, like through conditions of extreme poverty or ongoing abuse, then criminality or escape may be more likely.

Fifth. When other behaviours to change the bad life situation are unavailable or prohibited, normal behaviours get shaped into exaggerated forms and can have collateral effects. If these behaviours have a small effect and no alternatives arise, then they can become chronic should the situation continue. These behaviours might not have a direct or obvious connection to the bad life context, so we must be careful to avoid interpretation.

Sixth. The behaviours that become exaggerated are *not* of course random, but we know little yet about how they arise. People in bad life situations are shaped to try many different behaviours over time, never just one, but diagnoses ignore this. The behaviours which do occur need to be available and known to the person in the bad and inescapable life context (even if just through the media), and they need to have some effect even if it does not change what is bad in their situation.

While we need more contextual research with those who develop behaviours of mental health, the special conditions for these behaviours seem to be (1) normal responses to change bad life situations are not possible, (2) alternative strategies such as exiting are being blocked (usually by people), (3) if the bad situation is obvious and the opportunity is there, then other patterns of behaviours like criminality may occur, (4) but when the bad in the situation is not obvious, then normal behaviours which have some effect become exaggerated and locked in if the conditions continue, (5) what symptoms occur depends on what is available to that person. These properties together give the behaviours of mental health their surreal qualities, and the idea that they have seemingly sprung out of nowhere (or seem to be a brain malfunction).

Table 3.1 shows the main behaviours of the major DSM categories put into alphabetical order so that groupings are not made. The majority are normal behaviours, but which have been shaped into exaggeration or morphed into a new behaviour. We all do these behaviours in some form or another, and it was pointed out earlier that just observing the behaviour tells us nothing with the context.

Table 3.1 DSM-5 behaviours listed in alphabetical sequence. The behaviours found in the DSM-5 put into an alphabetical sequence, thereby making the list independent of disorders, in order to help reverse the intense categorisation learned from the DSM.

acute discomfort in close relationships	generalised anxiety	opposition behaviour
affective instability	grandiose ideas	orderliness preoccupation
agoraphobia	Grandiosity	Overactivity
anxiety, appear anxious or fearful	grossly disorganised or abnormal motor behaviour	overestimating threat
appear dramatic, emotional or erratic	Hallucinations	over-importance of thoughts
appear odd or eccentric	hallucinations or delusions	panic attacks
Argumentativeness	Hopelessness	perception disrupted from normal
attention seeking	hypersensitivity to negative evaluation	Perfectionism
being awake throughout the night, decreased sleep	identity disrupted from normal	perfectionism preoccupation
being reckless	Impulsivity	Phobias
body representation disrupted from normal	increased alcohol and drug use	Preoccupation
cognitive or perceptual distortions	increased energy	problems in the self-control of emotions that brings the individual into significant conflict
concentration difficulties	increased physical health complaints	racing thoughts
consciousness disrupted from normal	increased sex drive	rapid speech
crying spells	increased spending	recurrent and persistent thoughts
defiance	inflated sense of responsibility	repetitive behaviours applied rigidly
delusions	intermittent explosive anger	repetitive mental acts applied rigidly
desperation	intermittent explosive behaviours	restricted range of emotional expression

(Continued)

Table 3.1 (Continued)

detachment from social relationships	intermittent explosive irritation	sad mood, sadness
disorganised thinking	interpersonal relationships instability	self-control problems that bring the individual into significant conflict
disregard for the rights of others	intolerance of uncertainty	self-image instability
distrust and suspiciousness of others' motives	intrusive and unwanted thoughts	sleeping troubles
disturbance of eating, or eating-related behaviour	Irritability	slowing down of thoughts and actions
dysfunctional beliefs	lack of empathy	social inhibition
eccentricities of behaviour	lack of enjoyment, loss of interest in pleasurable activities	somatic changes that affect the individual's capacity to function
emotion disrupted from normal	memory disrupted from normal	spending less time with friends and family
empty mood	moodiness that is out of character	staying home from work or school
excessive emotionality	motor control disrupted from normal	submissive and clinging behaviour
excessive fear and anxiety	need for admiration	suicide thoughts
feeling overwhelmed	need to control thoughts	unable to adjust a particular stressor
feelings of inadequacy	negative symptoms	worry
finding it hard to take minor personal criticisms	Nervousness	

As a useful comparison, Table 3.2 shows the main behaviours which used to be diagnosed as '*hysteria*' in the late 1800s, taken from various authors.

Note the differences between Table 3.1 and Table 3.2, and compare these to the criteria in Box 3.1, especially point 6. The 1800s showed much less in the way of unusual language behaviours, and more physical behaviours, for example. The task is to relate these to what was 'available' or which had been modelled to these different groups of people. Is it perhaps that 'talking your way out' was not an option for the mainly working-class women who presented with these symptoms in the 1800s, meaning exaggerated language behaviours were simply not going to happen. There was also no wide social media from which people could learn other behaviours as happens now, we will see.

Alternative views of treatment and recovery

Since there are other books in this series on alternative views of mental health treatment (Guerin, 2017, 2020, 2022), it will not be covered in detail here, but any treatment clearly needs to focus on stopping or ameliorating the bad life

Table 3.2 The behaviours of 'hysteria' from the 1800s and early 1900s. Most older texts go on to classify these in some way, but we are interested in just the behaviours themselves. (assembled from Charcot, 1891, 1892; Janet, 1901, 1904, 1907; Scull, 2009)

loss of speech	all dramatic	'emotional' changes
loss of sight	fits	character changes
paralysis of hands, arms, legs	dramatic passions	suggestable
	no reactions if pricked or pinched	fixed and rigid ideas
inability to swallow		tics
'swelling' in abdomen or throat	not seeing or hearing	fits and attacks somnambulism
	difficulty attending	alternative states
sense of suffocation	weak memory	dissociation
odd breathing	laziness, hesitation	forgetfulness when out of alternative state
loss of sensations and reflexes	slowness, indecision	
	weakening or simplification of voluntary movements	alternative identities
odd facial expressions		tremors
odd postures	motor disturbances	eating problems
writhing	catalepsies	other senses disappear
vocal tics	rigidity of limbs	insensible patches on skin (used by witchfinders)
pains	loss of voice, hiccups, vomiting	
insensibilities		
palsy and contractions	memories of inflammation	
fainting	alterations of body, defects of anaesthesia	
one or both eyes blind		

situations of the person. This cannot be done by talking alone, as it requires a new way to think about treatments of mental health, learning from studies in criminality and other deviant behaviours (Maruna, 2007). It also cannot be done by a single person or therapist.

The outcomes of treatment will differ from those of the current mainstream medical and psychological models, as shown in Box 3.3 (Guerin, 2022). Medical models assume that a *cure* is the best outcome as defined when the behaviours *stop*. For a Social Contextual Analysis instead, *behaviours change when life contexts change*. This means that the behaviours do not disappear or get cured but are no longer shaped without their influencing contexts. Learned behaviours remain regardless of whether they are currently shaped into action or not, and many of the behaviours of 'mental health' are useful in some life situations. Those in therapy, especially for hearing voices, often remark that they do not want to get rid of the behaviours entirely but have them appear only when they are useful.

How to explore life contexts

What this approach means for both research and therapy is not to diagnose the behaviours of mental health into a medical taxonomy, but to find out the past and current life contexts for the person, and the links between these. This has to be far more detailed than the current client backgrounds carried out, although newer forms of formulations, some based on the Power Threat Meaning

Box 3.3 Successful therapy outcomes for medical models versus contextual approaches

Medical models of mental health	Contextual models of mental health
stop	disappear
are cured	become irrelevant
are blocked	become unnecessary
are corrected	go into the background
are fixed	fade away
	do not show up anymore (unless needed)
	can still be used in appropriate contexts
relapse means the behaviours were not properly cured	*relapse* means the original life contexts have returned

Framework, are better (Ball & Ritchie, 2021; Boyle & Johnstone, 2020; Johnstone, 2018; Johnstone & Dallos, 2014; La Roche & Bloom, 2018; Randall et al., 2020).

That, in a nutshell, is what this research and book are about. What can we learn from extensive conversations with nine women about their life contexts, and how these shaped their eating disorders and their recoveries? Chapter 15 will map out major findings alongside the contextual model of mental health from Box 3.1, but the case studies will focus on communicating the contextual details alone.

References

Ball, M., & Ritchie, R. (2021). *Suicide narratives: Healing through knowing.* Unpublished paper, Human Clinic.

Boyle, M., & Johnstone, L. (2020). *A straight talking introduction to the Power Meaning Threat Framework: An alternative to psychiatric diagnosis.* PCCS Books.

Charcot, J. M. (1891). *Traité de médecine* (Vol. 1). Masson.

Charcot, J. M. (1892). *Leçons du mardi à la Salpêtrière* (Vol. 1). Aux Bureau du Progrès Médical.

Guerin, B. (2017). *How to rethink mental illness: The human contexts behind the labels.* Routledge.

Guerin, B. (2020). *Turning mental health into social action.* Routledge.

Guerin, B. (2022). *Reimagining therapy through Social Contextual Analyses: Finding new ways to support people in distress.* Routledge.

Guerin, B., Thain, E., Stevens, K., Richards, A., & Leugi, G. B. (2024). *Doing contextual research: New ways to understand and influence yourself and other people.* Routledge.

Janet, P. (1901). *The mental state of hystericals.* Putnam's Sons. (Original works published in 1894).

Janet, P. (1904). Amnesia and the dissociation of memories by emotion. *Journal de Psychology, 1,* 417–453.

Janet, P. (1907). *The major symptoms of hysteria.* Macmillan.

Johnstone, L. (2018). Psychological formulation as an alternative to psychiatric diagnosis. *Journal of Humanist Psychology, 58,* 30–46.

Johnstone, L., Boyle, M., Cromby, J., Dillon, J., Harper, D., Kinderman, P., . . . Read, J. (2018). *The Power Threat Meaning Framework: Towards the identification of patterns in emotional distress, unusual experiences and troubled or troubling behaviour, as an alternative to functional psychiatric diagnosis.* British Psychological Society.

Johnstone, L., & Dallos, R. (Eds.). (2014). *Formulation in psychology and psychotherapy.* Routledge.

La Roche, M. J., & Bloom, J. B. (2018). Examining the effectiveness of the Cultural Formulation Interview with young children: A clinical illustration. *Transcultural Psychiatry, 45,* 1–16.

Maruna, S. (2007). *Making good: How ex-convicts reform and rebuild their lives.* American Psychological Association: Kindle Edition.

Maruna, S. (2008). *Making good: How ex-convicts reform and rebuild their lives.* APA.

Randall, J., Johnson, E., & Johnstone, L. (2020). Self-formulation: Making sense of your own experiences. In J. Randall (Ed.), *Surviving clinical psychology: Navigating personal, professional and political selves on the journey to qualification* (pp. 142–164). Routledge.

Scull, A. (2009). *Hysteria: The disturbing history.* Oxford University Press.

4 What our research was about and introducing our nine collaborators

The approach we took and why

While social contexts are paramount in understanding the behaviours of eating disorders, the current mainstream explanations oversimplify social context through the abstract bio-psycho-social models, and the research measures little of this. In the previous chapter we saw the limitations of past research, which consists mostly of brief cross-sectional studies, with most of the theorising having been abstract and not observable. We also know that current treatments based on this research are not working well with low recovery and high relapse.

Our approach therefore sought to discover as much about the participant's life context as possible in order to show how eating disorder behaviours are shaped in diverse ways (Box 3.1). This methodology differs from those in psychology but has similarities with other social sciences, especially social anthropology.

To best meet these aims, informal and repeated conversations with each participant were conducted, which followed the *conversational* approach outlined by Guerin et al. (2018) and Guerin et al. (2024). An unstructured interview style allowed participants to elaborate or deviate, while iterative questioning allowed the researcher to learn the frank details beyond initial more abstract narratives. The research questions for this study were left open-ended to capture the diversity and variability in participants' stories, rather than finding common themes and generalising women with eating disorders. The aim of this study was to gain detailed contexts from a small sample and avoid generalisation, thus only nine participants formed our group (Guerin et al., 2018).

What we asked

The stories for this book came from three different projects with different research questions, but which all followed the same methodology and discovered contexts around the development and recovery of eating disorders. We began by asking the participants to describe their life generally and let stories about their eating disorder arise naturally. Informal questioning was done by the researcher

DOI: 10.4324/9781003453918-5

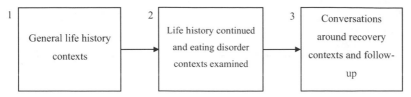

Figure 4.1 A generic interview process done over several conversations

for clarification and to learn more contextual details. We wanted to know the social, economic, environmental, historical and cultural contexts during their early lives, and how these contexts changed over time.

Repeat interviews were done with each woman, as multiple conversations have advantages for any research (Guerin et al., 2018, 2024). Follow-up sessions spanned many weeks and sometimes months. This meant we could ask for further aspects of contexts after digesting what had been said in a previous conversation, and typically the women would recall more contextual details before the following session. Many significant events were not brought up until hours of talking had passed, and later narratives had more nuance than earlier narratives.

Figure 4.1 gives the rough idea of how these multiple conversations progressed but each one turned out differently as they were primarily driven by the women and their stories, not by us.

The interviews were audio recorded with permission so that they could be analysed by the primary researcher and relevant parts transcribed. The data were not analysed for common themes or for the number of times something was mentioned, as is done in other research. Analysis required looking past repetition of abstract language and looking for frank or concrete descriptions of what happened. Sometimes contextual details were offered clearly and once was enough. Other times the researcher needed to draw together different clues across the conversations to present the context. There was no standard method that could be followed to analyse the data, because their stories and lives were too unique and complex. For privacy and confidentiality, the recordings were only available to the primary researcher, and the conversations were too rich to transcribe in total. Therefore, what is presented and compared in this book was dependent on what the primary researchers brought from their project; however, the team continued to deepen the contextual analysis by liaising with the primary researcher.

Our collaborators/participants

There were nine cis gendered women engaged in conversation for this research. To protect their identities, they were all given pseudonyms and any identifying details have been disguised. The names they were assigned are listed, followed by the primary interviewer in brackets.

Katrina	Sally	Gabby	(Millie Tait)
Adora	Bianca	Courtney	(Scarlett Kraehe)
Diane	Erica	Fiona	(Nikia Bailey)

Some more details are given in Table 4.1, including their ages, their labelled diagnoses, how they were interviewed and how long they were interviewed.

Ethics: How did we treat the women?

The University of South Australia Human Research Ethics Committee approved the researchers to talk to women (1) previously diagnosed with an eating disorder, (2) over the age of 18, (3) not currently in a crisis of any sort and (4) who considered themselves recovered or in the process of recovery. Specific diagnoses were unimportant due to the fundamental overlap in eating disorder behaviours, and recovery was self-defined due to the complex and ambiguous nature of eating disorder recovery.

Table 4.1 Some details of the nine participants and their conversations with us.

Pseudonym	Age (at the time of interview)	Eating disorder diagnosis	Method of conversation	Number of conversations	Total time of conversations
Adora	54	Bulimia nervosa	Face-to-face	3	3h 40m
Bianca	21	Unspecified eating disorder	Face-to-face	3	4h 10m
Courtney	32	Bulimia nervosa	Video chat	4	4h 42m
Diane	21	Anorexia nervosa	Face-to-face and video chat	3	7h 32m
Erica	21	Anorexia nervosa	Face-to-face	3	8h 14m
Fiona	21	Anorexia nervosa	Face-to-face	4	8h 52m
Katrina	29	AFRID and anorexia nervosa. Identifies with orthorexia.	Video chat	3	5h
Gabby	30	Anorexia nervosa. Periodically purging.	Face-to-face	3	7h
Sally	25	Not formally diagnosed. Identifies with anorexia nervosa. Periodically purging.	Video chat	3	7h 21m

How did we locate these nine women?

The participants were recruited by 'snowballing' from the researchers' existing networks, which facilitated quick rapport and retention of participants. To reduce any conflicts of interests this was ideally done through the distribution of an information sheet to third-party individuals known to the interviewer, who then passed it on to potential participants unfamiliar to the interviewer. However, other participants were recruited by informal promotion through the researcher's existing networks which did recruit some acquaintances already known by the researcher to have lived experience. But these participants did not share current or ongoing contexts with the researcher.

Prior to the interviews, participants were briefed about the terms and risks of participation and then asked to provide written consent. Participants were advised to only answer questions they felt comfortable answering, and they could withdraw from the study at any point. They were given a gift card regardless of how long they spoke for or how many sessions they attended. Following each session, participants were invited to attend follow-up sessions but were not obliged and could withdraw.

The women's stories

The women's stories are long and complex which reflects the reality of how eating disorders occur (Guerin, 2020). There is a need to get away from assuming there is a single causal path that determines the complex behaviours flippantly labelled as 'eating disorders'. There is no magic bullet as an explanation. So, no apology is made for giving long stories, because the answers lie in the details.

Although there are key points that will be summarised in Chapters 14 and 15, each woman's story was very different.

A note about the quotes

The quotes published in this book have been edited slightly to include more content and to improve reading flow, but we have been careful to do so without changing the original meaning of the speaker. Some of the changes we have made:

- Stutters and some 'filler' words have been removed such as: *like, you know, yeah, um.*
- Identifying information like names and places has been removed.
- Words in [square brackets] have been included to give the reader context.
- Ellipses (. . .) have been used to stitch together relevant quotes about events or context.
- Ellipses (. . .) have been used to remove excess words.

References

Guerin, B. (2020). *Turning mental health into social action*. Routledge.

Guerin, B., Leugi, G. B., & Thain, A. (2018). Attempting to overcome problems shared by both qualitative and quantitative methodologies: Two hybrid procedures to encourage diverse research. *The Australian Community Psychologist, 29*(2), 74.

Guerin, B., Thain, E., Stevens, K., Leugi, G., & Richards, A. (2024). *How to conduct contextual research: Finding out about yourself and other people*. Routledge.

Part 2

The unusual eating behaviours of our nine collaborators

5 Adora's story
Becoming a "good girl"

Adora's eating disorder was centred around her playing the role of "good girl" in her community. Her story will explore the contextual nuances that shaped this role and how it changed across her life. The following quote summarises how integral this role has been in shaping her behaviour over time and will be elaborated on throughout.

> *I've always thought that I'm very unlovable . . . my whole life I have wanted to . . . prove that I'm a good girl so that people will love me . . . [So], what's a good girl? . . . She's someone that's never angry, she's someone that puts her needs last, never hurts other people's feelings, she's someone who is feminine . . . is very thin and eats like a bird . . . I've come up with this fantasy thing of what a good girl is . . . and that's what I'm trying to prove to the world.*

Early life contexts

Adora's contextual underpinnings begin with her conception. She was conceived out of wedlock in a very conservative family, and her two young parents got married to maintain their status in the community. Adora had to be perfect to counteract the shame her birth brought upon the family.

> *[I] came along when mum was 18 . . . and they got married because they were pregnant with me. And it was very shameful.*
> *I had to be the successful child . . . [that was] pretty, well behaved, good child— girl. To prove that they got married for the right reasons and they stayed together.*

Family values: How to be a good girl

Overt cultural discourses around family responsibilities were salient in Adora's formation of her self. Being a good girl was heavily enforced by her maternal grandmother towards both Adora and her mother.

> *My nanna always said to me, and she said it to my mum as well, 'You have to be a good girl or I won't love you'. . . . I'm always wanting to make sure that . . . I'm*

DOI: 10.4324/9781003453918-7

not offending anybody. And I have to be super, super kind and nice and thoughtful and always the most helpful person in the room.

Adora was an extension of her parents' reputation in the community. Adora's parents shaped her environment by enrolling her in a private school and extra-curricular classes to ensure she had the resources to become the good girl they wanted her to be.

> *I think a lot of the conditioning that I got from my mum and dad—who got it from their parents . . . I was trying to fit in, but they were trying to fit in too, and they wanted me to fit in . . . mum wanted me to be something I was never going to be.*
>
> *[Mum] had aspirations for me to be the tennis player and the ballerina, she took me to ballet classes, and I persisted 'til I was 15. . . . She sent me to elocution lessons to try and get me to be good at public speaking, and I was mortified. It was a round peg in a square hole . . . she wanted to give me the opportunity that she never had . . . and she looked at her other friends' kids and wanted me to be like them . . . it's that classic thing that parents do. Instead of wanting your kid to grow up to be themselves . . . your children become a bit of an accessory. Someone to show off.*

Adora's parents' relationship and values surrounding marriage also shaped the way Adora understood what was expected of her later in her life.

> *Mum and dad's relationship . . . was a product of its time . . . mum is the 'inno-cent, dependent, submissive woman', and my dad is the 'in-control provider, caller of the shots', makes all the decisions, continually makes sarcastic jives at everyone to keep them in their place. Mum thinks it's hilarious, but it's not, it's actually really rude. And it hurts mum a lot as well. She tries to pretend that she just thinks it's funny. . . .*

Food consumption as a life-or-death behaviour

When Adora was 5 years old, she found her mother unconscious following an attempted suicide. Meeting her mother's expectations and avoiding disappointing her became a way to protect them both from her mother's suicide.

> *I always protected my mother, and I still do . . . and it comes back to the fact that when I was 5 . . . she overdosed . . . and I found her on the floor, with tablets all around her . . .*

So, when Adora's brother refused to eat and caused their mother distress, Adora ate her whole plate of food without complaints and cherished the praise that came from this. Adora learnt how eating could affect other people and also change the way they responded to her.

> *When I was growing up there was just me and my brother, and my brother would refuse to eat whatever my mum cooked every single night, and mum would always*

end up in tears. So, food was a very emotive, powerful thing . . . and I used to eat everything up . . . and I do remember the first time I ate everything off my plate and how much praise I got. . . . I was only, I reckon about 5 or 6, 'cause I remember . . . finishing everything on my plate and getting praise and going, 'Oh' and that sticks in my mind . . . whereas . . . my younger brother caused lots of havoc.

Adora began to understand the emotional responses people could have to food consumption. It could affect how people viewed her, or how they acted as a response to these behaviours. She learned that she could use this behaviour to seek praise, while avoiding criticism.

How to look like a good girl

Adora began to draw more and more from the discourses of her community to better understand what was expected of her. She realised that being a good girl was much more than good manners when she observed her family scrutinise women's bodies, especially women in bigger bodies. She began to understand that it was her duty to ensure she never became fat as this may affect her integrity and by extension, that of her parents.

From a very, very early age, it was all about what I look like, and also I think, within all families, but especially—definitely in my grandparent's family, and in my regular family . . . you're not worthy unless you're attractive . . . and you're not worthy if you're overweight. And, a beautiful person, it is virtuous . . . all the values . . . all the beautiful human virtues are associated with attractive people.

One of the things my dad always said was, 'Oh, she's got a big arse, fat arse—fat arse, fat arse, fat arse'. Having a big bum was like, a major crime. . . . So, I always look at my bum and think, 'Is it big? Is it big? Is it big?' . . .

I just don't want anyone looking at me and walking away thinking, 'Oh, god, look at that'. Like . . . my dad did constantly . . . and my dad, still to this day, fat-shames everyone around.

Development of eating disorder

New community, new experiences, same ideals

Adora attended an all-girls school from the age of 12, where the thin-ideal of her family was observed amongst her peers, who provided Adora with a more tangible idea of what the thin-ideal should look like and what behaviours she could use to achieve this.

All the girls just looked at each other and criticised or praised each other . . . it was all about how you looked. . . . I remember . . . a group of us walking to the swimming pool, and everyone was saying, 'Oh, look at her, that's amazing, imagine knowing that you haven't got an ounce of fat on your body'. And I remember thinking, 'Huh? Ah, is that what we should be doing?' and I just went, 'Ah, okay', because it was anything to fit in, because . . . I was never in the popular crowd and rejected by my good-looking friends. . . . And so I was always trying to—'What can I do to fit in?' So . . . that inspired me, in the wrong way.

It was not just discussions about body-image and weight-loss that affected Adora's behaviours. At the age of 14, she was coerced by her boyfriend into having sex for the first time. Shortly after this, her eating disorder behaviours began to arise.

The first time I had sex the boy sort of forced me into it. . . . I was going out with him so . . . he was drunk, and I was like, 'Oh, no, no, no'. And then that's it. And after that, was sort of like, 'Oh whatever'. . . .

I remember the next day going to my girlfriend's and saying, 'I'm not a virgin, we had sex last night'. . . . I was the first one, and it felt like I had achieved something that they hadn't. . . . I didn't explain to them how it actually happened.

Adora used the story of her sexual experience as a social resource, eagerly telling her friends at school. However, she later felt that he gave her "the creeps" and decided to break up with him soon after this happened. Shortly after this, her eating disorder behaviours began.

He was really wanting to stay with me, and I was like, 'Ugh, no', he gave me the creeps. . . .

I think he probably didn't [give me the creeps] before [we had sex] . . . [I broke up with him] not long after that. I didn't really connect the two. I think I did take responsibility . . . I think it is a classic case of me saying, 'Well, I didn't oppose him strongly enough. And I should have got out of there'.

It probably did coincide with all of that [eating disorder] . . . it was around the same time, come to think of it. . . .

Adora did not understand the sinister nature of this sexual experience as there was very little discourse in her world that could help her contextualise it. There was, however, likely discussions about sex being something for adults, and while Adora felt "creeped out" after this, it was also an adult behaviour. Being forced to please a man did not seem strange, as Adora had spent her whole life with adults who perpetuated a patriarchal power dynamic in which her mother's behaviours socially elevated her father. This could be considered an integral introduction into womanhood for Adora.

It's only really, as an adult, that you hear other people's stories and you think, 'Oh, actually, he forced me to'. . . . We're so much more aware now . . . if that happened to me now, it would not be okay. But at that age, and in that time, I didn't even think about the fact that it was really almost a date rape thing.

How to be a good girl in womanhood

Adora had spent her life surrounded by discourse that praised women for being thin and beautiful; however, it was not until she began to understand herself as a woman that she began to act accordingly. Her new identity of woman came after she began puberty and then had sex for the first time. Adora had to balance the discourse of womanhood alongside her good girl role. Adora mimicked the weight-loss behaviours that were discussed by her peers in an attempt to fit into society.

> *I just watched people around me . . . some of the really popular girls get really skinny and I started to copy them. And I think when your body starts to develop, I started to worry that it was going to get too big.*

For Adora, weight-loss was not about beauty; it was a way for her to avoid being observed. She had learnt from her family that women could be scrutinised for being "too fat" or "disgusting", so, losing weight, and wearing loosely fitting, neutral coloured clothing were behaviours to help her "blend in". By avoiding attention, she could continue to be a polite and nice girl as she entered into womanhood, not a woman with a "big bum" who was unworthy of love.

> *I hate my face . . . I don't even think about my face. But I can control my body—to some extent. So, I'm comparing my weight to another person's, and my body shape.*
> *I've always just worn really baggy clothes because I just don't want anyone looking at me and walking away thinking, 'Oh, god, look at that'.*

Food consumption: A socially strategic behaviour

Adora matched her eating behaviours with her immediate audience, so she was able to please both family and peers. She would eat breakfast and dinner at home with her family and then reduce her intake while she was at school away from her mother's surveillance.

> *I would have breakfast and then at recess time I had nothing but I would drink lots and lots and lots and lots of lots of water, fill up on water. And at lunchtime, I can't remember what I had. Probably . . . just the usual sausage-roll or something like that. . . . And then just had dinner with everyone at home.*

Unsurprisingly, Adora began to struggle with her restrictive food consumption, which ultimately led her to begin binge eating. However, through those around her, she was taught to purge her food.

> *I would just eat less and less . . . and lost lots of weight, and then . . . it led to bingeing, because I was starving, and then I . . . heard someone say, 'Oh, just throw it up'. And [I thought], 'Ah, that's a brilliant idea!' so then it turned into bulimia.*

Purging is often a behaviour that is done in secret; however, even secret behaviours are social in nature. They can be done to achieve a socially desirable result, such as weight-loss, or spoken about for a variety of reasons. In this case, purging served as a resource that was given to Adora by her friend.

How do good girls take control?

Adora was never taught how to deal with her conflicts directly, nor was she given any control within her household. She was, however, taught that she could use eating behaviours to gain a sense of control and power when her brother refused food in childhood. Controlling her food intake became a way for her to deal with conflict without compromising her good girl status.

> *And it gives you a big power kick, right? Knowing that you're not eating and almost feeling superior to other people.*
>
> *I can remember it happening when I was with my family . . . my mum and my dad, and they were driving me crazy. And I'd sit there shovelling food into my face, and then going to the toilet and throwing up, and then coming out again and then having to listen to their bullshit, whatever it was, and then, shovelling more food in and going and throwing it up and coming back. And it was almost an anger that I couldn't express, in an adaptive way . . . [I] never had the skills to sort of say what I was feeling, probably didn't even know what I was feeling anyway. And so I ended up just eating and then throwing up and feeling a sense of real relief and release . . . and it made me really think, 'This is making me sick. You guys make me sick'.*

Adora's behaviours were cultural; she learnt them from the people around her who were also doing these behaviours to help them deal with their environments. The eating disorder expressed her agency while also fitting in with peers at school and family members at home.

> *I went to a school where . . . eating disorders were the coping mechanism for some sort of mental ill health. . . . But if I'd gone to a school where everyone was drinking, or smoking dope or, whatever, I might have ended up smoking drugs or . . . getting hooked on ice or something. . . . But that was the . . . culturally accepted maladaptive behaviour . . . my theory is that we've all got these things that we're dealing with, and we're all navigating . . . this weird life, and it just depends on where you are as to what maladaptive behaviour you may or may not pick up.*

Changing contexts, changing behaviours

Adora's eating disorder behaviours remained consistent for a couple of years but became progressively worse when she was 16 years old. Around this time, Adora's sister was born which was a major change within the household, and Adora's role changed once again. She was no longer the only daughter and, being a young woman, she no longer required the same level of surveillance from her parents that she once received. These changes resulted in Adora feeling less powerful within her household.

> *I have sometimes wondered to myself, whether that was me as a jealous teenager, being replaced by a young girl . . . I think it became part of my identity . . . It gave me a sense of power and control . . . that I didn't feel that I had. . . .*
>
> *There wasn't that much attention anyway, really. . . . We weren't really a close family at that time.*

Adora had more opportunity to do eating disorder behaviours because her parents were preoccupied with their new baby. On one occasion, she left evidence of her vomit in the bathroom. This allowed Adora to control her mother's emotions in a way that was safe for her and her mother as she was only revealing an indication of her behaviour to provoke a reaction.

> *I remember, mum got cross once because she found some vomit in the toilet. And she said, 'Someone's been sick in there' . . . whether I wanted her to find out . . . I don't know what I was thinking.*

Recovery

Eventually, Adora did tell her mother about her eating disorder, but she did not initially believe her because Adora had kept this behaviour so well hidden. Adora had to tell her mother and the doctor the extent of her behaviour before they expressed some concern.

> *I went to my mum and went to the doctor . . . mum took me seriously enough to take me to the doctor, but she was a bit angry with me more than anything. And then the doctor said, 'You're just . . . eating the tails off the lamb chops'. . . . And when I said, 'No, no, I'm, sometimes I make myself throw up like four or five times a day'. And they went like 'Oh?'*

A new "framework to live by"

Adora was referred to a psychiatrist who encouraged her to join group therapy, where she learnt some life-changing skills and outlooks that helped her better understand her environment. Of particular importance to Adora was the introduction of feminism.

> *[My psychiatrist] put me in touch with a psych nurse . . . and she was a feminist and sort of opened my eyes to that stuff. And then I started reading . . . 'Fat Is a Feminist Issue' by Susie Orbach. . . . That was a life-changing thing. In fact, I think I read that book many, many, many times, as a bit of a lifeline. But then . . . they put me in with a group of about six other women, who all had varying types of eating disorders . . . we would just do group therapy . . . they would throw in feminists perspectives . . . and I think that turned things around for me.*

Feminist discourses allowed Adora to better understand the contexts around her and how they shaped the behaviours and values of the communities she was living in. This allowed her to reframe her body-image concerns as being a discourse, stemming from the social and historical contexts that have harboured the patriarchal society she was, and continues living in. So, while her contexts did not change, her discourse surrounding these contexts allowed her to experience some liberation from the constraints they had on her life. They were no longer something she understood as an internal stress and became an external issue.

> *It gave me a perspective to function through daily life with. So, I didn't have to be the pretty, feminine girl. . . . I could just do what I was comfortable with . . . and focus on what I thought was more important . . . feminism gave me a way of living according to healthier values. So, when I'm faced with bullshit in the media, feminism gives me a way of navigating that. And even . . . my thoughts sometimes, the feminist stuff gives me a framework to live by.*

"Sitting pretty" with nowhere to go

Therapy was important in Adora's recovery, but she continued to live with her parents and depend on them for resources. Her powerlessness seemed much bigger now that Adora was older and aware of global discourses. She began to comprehend the magnitude of suffering and inequalities happening around the world while she was "sitting pretty", surrounded by an abundance of resources. However, she had no power over how these resources were distributed.

> *I'd had a big fight with dad. We were watching, I think Ethiopia were going through a bad time and . . . we were sitting pretty in this house, and [I] said, 'Dad, can we donate some money?' [He said], 'Oh no. . . . ', and I just went to my room and overdosed . . . then in the morning they found me and I'd just thrown it all up. And, they just cleaned it up and whatever.*

The message from her family was that a good girl was "someone that . . . puts her needs last, never hurts other people's feelings", but when her father denied her request to help others, she realised that the resources her parents were giving her were not to serve what *she wanted* but instead what they *wanted her to want*. This new comprehension of powerlessness was something that Adora could not compensate for with her eating behaviours, and so instead, she attempted suicide through overdose, much like her mother had done years ago.

"Sitting [not-so-] pretty" on the road to liberation

Adora began to truly recover when she moved out of home at the age of 18, following a suggestion from her counsellor. Adora's mother's family dealt with conflict by avoiding future interactions. So, moving was instrumental in maintaining her relationship with her mother as it reduced the likelihood of conflict arising.

Mum and me . . . we were obviously not getting along . . . we didn't have lots and lots of fights or anything, but . . . we don't do conflict very well. People tend to have a fight and they never talk to each other again, in mum's family . . . it didn't take much conflict—and then [my counsellor] suggested moving out. . . .

Adora's father supported her move, by buying her a car and employing her as a cleaner at his factory. This allowed Adora to be independent financially as well as giving her access to independent travel, something she did not have prior to this.

I was saying, 'Look, I'm going to move out'. And dad took me aside and said, 'Okay, well, I'll give you a job'.—he had a factory, and I used to do the cleaning there every Saturday and he generously paid me for that and it was enough for me to—but I also had a waitressing job. . . . Moving out was the best thing that I ever did . . . because I had the job, I was actually [able to support myself], and I lived off the smell of an oily rag. So, I never ever, ever asked them for any more money.

Adora could fund her recovery which allowed her greater choice. She commenced 'antidepressants' which her parents had previously declined on her behalf. While the medication likely had some pharmaceutical benefits, it was also a way to assert her agency and defy her parents, something she was only able to do through eating disorder behaviours previously.

Mum and dad didn't want me to go on antidepressants, 'cause there was still . . . a stigma associated with antidepressants. . . . So they said 'no' and to be honest that was probably the biggest gift they gave me 'cause I just went, 'Oh, yes, I will . . .' when I started taking them, and I probably didn't look back after that. I think the medication was definitely the turning point.

Adora's new environments meant that she was no longer surrounded by the same magnitude of body-image discourse that shaped her eating disorder behaviours. She was instead able to embrace the feminist perspectives she had learned about at the beginning of her recovery.

I gave up [trying to be an attractive woman] as soon as I left home . . . which was really nice actually. And that was the feminist thing . . . I cut my hair short, and I didn't wear makeup. . . . I always had all my body hair. . . . That was very liberating . . . but then the weight was still a thing, but I . . . sort of just gradually learnt how to navigate society—our community in my own way.

Passing the spotlight

Adora's parents expected her to be an extraverted socialite, but she never wanted to be in the spotlight. This pressure followed her throughout her childhood and teenage years until her younger sister grew up and eagerly filled this role.

I had a sister who loved to be the centre of attention. And we had a conversation where I said, 'Oh, when I walk in a room I just want to blend in. I don't want anyone to look at me, and think, "Oh my god, look at her". Or, "Oh wow, look at her!" I don't want either of those comments. I just want to be camouflaged and just blend in', and she said, 'Oh, really? Oh no, when I walk in a room, I want everyone to look at me'.

The pressure was off when [my sister] came along because [she] was perfect. . . .

Navigating life after recovery

As Adora entered her 20s, she began to navigate her life post-eating disorder. She attended university to study early childhood and started her career as a teacher; fell in love with and married her husband; and had two children. Her life was full of new relationships and contexts which allowed her to establish the autonomy she craved as a teenager, and yet, she still engaged in fluctuating disordered eating.

Family, it's what's familiar . . .

Familial contexts: Adora's relationship with her parents had changed drastically, because her parents had two more children and were busy raising three very young children during Adora's 20s. However, their expectations of her were still prevalent when they did see her, particularly when it came to her relationship.

I went out with [my now husband] . . . I had short hair . . . I didn't wear a scrap of makeup . . . we all went out to dinner, and I put on a dress—for some reason—and afterwards, mum said to me, 'Aw [your father] . . . he's so happy that . . . you're making yourself look good'. . . . It was all about what I looked like, at all times.

When Adora did get married at the age of 22, her family were glad to see her acting in a way that aligned with their ideas of a good girl. This brought with it reiterations of other good girl values such as being thin.

Nanna and Pop . . . when I had my wedding . . . Nanna very kindly helped fix up my wedding dress and they said, 'Oh yes, you're a good coat hanger'. And I said, 'What do you mean?' and they said, 'Oh, you look good with the clothes on'.

Familial behaviours: When placed in these familial contexts with her family, Adora's eating disorder behaviours often resurfaced as a way for her to assert some control without causing conflict.

In years gone by, I would have gone [to a family event], not really prepared myself, got wound up by something people were talking about, or judgments they were making, overeaten, gone and thrown up in the bathroom, come out, eaten more, gone and thrown up in the bathroom again . . . and then just been exhausted for the next few days . . . it's a bit of a theme, not being able to say what I'm thinking . . . conflict in a reasonable manner. It's too hard. So, then I just abuse myself and throw up, and go away feeling really angry.

My psychiatrist used to say to me, 'Food's your friend, it's your friend that you go to, to soothe yourself'. And it was, it was a soothing thing. He said my maladaptive relationship with food was my little thing I could go to . . . to help me feel better. Like a drug.

Familial values, "It's worth more than anything": While Adora's eating disorder behaviours reduced, her thoughts regarding her body remained unchanged. These thoughts were particularly rampant before and during seeing people, such as her family, who had previously made negative comments about other people's bodies.

There are a number of people in my life that I don't see that often. Or if I do see them, I think to myself, 'Oh God, have I put on weight? I haven't seen them for a while. Are they going to notice?' Or, 'Oh good, I've lost weight, they'll think I'll look good. . . . This is good, I'm glad that I'm a bit thinner now'. And it's usually only a matter of a few kilos. . . .

She still thought that all of her unhappiness would cease if she had the 'perfect body'. So, even though she was no longer clinically diagnosable, her thoughts remained thin-centric.

I have this fantasy that I've got no cellulite, and I look, and I think, 'If I didn't have cellulite, would I not be as unhappy with my body?' And I think perhaps . . . I would be much happier—if I had beautiful honey gold skin, with no freckles, and just . . . then I would be happy, you know . . . like, if I see . . . beautiful women . . . they're lucky enough to have no cellulite. I just stare at them longingly, like, 'Oh my god, it would be amazing to have legs like that. . . . ' It's worth more than anything.

"I didn't have any serious relapses . . . oh, hang on . . ."

Adora continued to value weight-loss, and when she unintentionally lost weight while breastfeeding her child, she was thrilled by what this meant socially. Despite this excitement, Adora's behaviours did not become exaggerated into a 'disorder' again.

I didn't have any serious relapses . . . oh, hang on actually, when I was breastfeeding [my son]—And I did it for a year, I was working full time, 'cause I went back when he was 6 months old. . . . So, I got extremely thin there. But that was purely because of the breastfeeding . . . some people, if you're breastfeeding and working full time. . . . It just sucks . . . the life out of you. And I became so thin . . . I was underweight. But it wasn't deliberate. . . . At first, I was just too preoccupied [to care]. As time went on, though, and I got well, and I was still slim. I loved that . . . . that was a pretty good time . . . I remember feeling quite attractive and wearing nice clothes and feeling a bit more confident. And, when I had [my daughter] and was able to lose weight again after that . . . because I went back to work again . . . I was really slender there for a while, and I did love it. I loved it.

I don't think they ever became seriously disordered. I just sort of had. . . . It's just this low line . . . concerns that are always there.

New methods for handling trauma

From her late 20s onwards, as she navigated raising two children and working full time, Adora's methods for dealing with bad life situations had evolved. Her behaviours were now what could be better described, in diagnostic terms, as depression. She became more avoidant, and she began to experience ruminations, often in the form of suicidal ideation.

If I'm well, I can distract myself with healthy interactions, healthy behaviours, healthy thoughts. . . . But if I'm not well, then it just takes over and I can't seem to distract myself or get out of it, and I end up going down a deep, dark well . . . and I think, 'Oh everyone just hates me, I'm so repulsive'. . . . When I'm in that zone, the rumination gets out of control . . . of course, one thought leads to another, that's when I end up just having suicidal ruminations and . . . I think the only way to make it stop . . . would be to die.

Sad news, such as her sister completing suicide when Adora was 36, elicited negative internal discourse. However, her thoughts were not vocalised or acted on because of what this would mean socially, particularly now that she was a mother. Unlike eating disorder behaviours, secret suicidal thoughts did not interfere with her ability to look after her family or work full time.

I had kids by then. . . . And god, I was too busy working full time and raising two kids and doing the rest.

Her sister's suicide also changed the way that Adora's family interacted as they became more affectionate towards one another.

Since [my sister] died, we're much closer. When we were younger . . . no one said, 'I love you'. And no one gave hugs or anything like that. But now we're very huggy and [say], 'I love you'. . . . So, yeah, it did bring us closer.

Recent years

History echoing: "I sound like my dad, . . . but I never say it out loud"

. . . to this day, whenever I pick up a biscuit, I always remember my dad saying, 'Oh, you'll end up the size of a house'.

While Adora identifies as being fully recovered, much of her thinking is shaped by the discourses that nurtured her eating disorder decades ago. After 30 years of recovery, Adora's fear of weight-gain remains just as poignant.

> *It's interesting how much time and energy I waste on what I eat, what I look like, and definitely looking at other people constantly. . . . If I compare favourably, I get 'Ah' a sense of relief and if I compare unfavourably, I feel ashamed of myself- and immediately think, 'They must think I'm disgusting'. . . . I hadn't even realised I was doing it, it's just part of my existence. . . .*
>
> *. . . There's a deep, deep fear, that's never gonna go away, that if I get fat, no one's gonna like me. . . . I would rather kill myself than get fat. I've never said this to anyone before. I would rather do anything than get fat. . . . I don't know how people can go on living if they're fat.*

However, the discourse that Adora vocalises to others is body-positive and shaped by feminist perspectives. This is a far more positive social behaviour that aligns with her good girl values. Letting people know how much she thinks about body-image could make her seem rude or self-obsessed, not traits that a good girl should possess.

> *I'm really ashamed of these fat-shaming opinions and judgments that I have. I sound like my father and I sound like other people I know who do it out loud, but I never say it out loud. . . . Usually, no matter what I'm thinking, I'll just say, 'You're gorgeous . . . you're curvy'.*
>
> *I always tell stories to make myself look good. . . . I'm trying to make myself seem like a good person . . . so I'm always telling stuff about— 'Oh, I've done that. I'm gonna do this. I'm gonna do that'. And it's pretty exhausting.*
>
> *I just think they'd see me for—superficial, vain, insipid, pathetic . . . preoccupied-with-stupid-things person . . . that I can be. . . .*

New discourse audiences

Adora has learned methods to cope with these discourses when they happen around her, reframing them through discourse by making them comical with her friends. She also has thoughts that occur for the audience of her late sister, and uses these thought conversations to challenge the discourse silently.

> *When men . . . say that sort of thing [fat-shaming women] . . . dad, and men like that . . . I try to say something to them, but mostly I think, 'This is gonna make a good story, I can't wait to tell . . . [my best friend]'.*
>
> *I always talk to my dead sister, and say, '. . . just help me get through this without reacting or getting defensive, and help me just be positive'. . . . But these days I seem to be managing it better—I think I've got people, I just go away, and I think, 'I can't wait to tell . . . [my best friend] about that one'. . . .*

What we can learn from Adora

Adora's story is defined by an overwhelming desire to be a good girl. Her behaviours changed across her lifetime in response to the behaviours and discourses around her. In the 21st Century, there is so much content that young people constantly have access to which may mean that they do not recall when they realised that "women should be thin", or learnt about vomiting after eating, or overdosing to complete suicide. They have likely seen or heard about these behaviours online, on television, in a magazine or through another person who has seen or heard about it online, on television, in a magazine. Whereas, Adora knew women should be thin from the discourse at home and at school; she knew how to have an eating disorder from school; she knew about suicide through overdose from her mother. These behaviours were learnt through her environment and then elicited in response to her environment. Adora's story showcases the way in which behaviours can be understood through external events and contexts, rather than being purely cognitive.

Even as Adora enters her adult years and her depression overtakes her eating disorder, her thoughts are still being shaped by her history of conflict resolution behaviours: suicide. And her reasons for ruminating about this behaviour are because she is so worried about not being a good girl. Another indicator of her environmental influence is her sister's suicide. It is not my intention to blame anyone for this tragic event, but there is a theme in this family that suggests something in their environment makes dealing with bad life events difficult; whether this is solely related to conflict resolution, it is not clear.

Adora offered so much thoughtful insight on her behaviours and environment, and even provided me with new perspectives for my research.

6 Gabby's story

A ballerina's sacrifice

Gabby kept her eating disorder a secret until she was detained and diagnosed at the age of 22. Gabby was diagnosed with bipolar and anorexia nervosa, and she understood these to be two different illnesses that interacted. She associated fatness with being out of control, depressed and not doing well. Being thin was deemed necessary in her pursuit of being a professional ballerina, which she had been training for since she was 5 years old. Gabby said how she loved ballet from the first lesson because it connected with her perfectionist personality, and she put pressure on herself to achieve high standards. When Gabby became unwell and could no longer pursue ballet, her efforts to lose weight did not cease. For Gabby, recovery meant stabilising both her depression and eating disorder through medication, treatment and finding motivation to get better. But through our conversations we learnt more about the hidden contexts of her "really good, really normal" life that shaped the development and recovery of her eating disorder.

Childhood and primary school

"I suddenly had this awareness of like 'I'm fat'"

At 8 years old, Gabby began to judge her body as being "fat". When her mother was alerted to Gabby's self-criticism and queried her, Gabby realised this was not what the adults wanted to hear, so she kept those thoughts a secret.

> *Something in my head just went, 'Oh, you have to lie', like, 'No, I'm not fat', I just told her like, 'No', even though in my head I thought that. . . . I was just like, 'Oh, I can't tell people things like that because they get worried, so I have to keep this to myself, this is a secret'.*

DOI: 10.4324/9781003453918-8

"[Mum] doesn't live in the moment a lot. She's always like, 'What's the next thing? What are we doing here?' So we're not very good at just chilling"

Gabby's parents both worked outside of normal business hours, and her mother took minimal maternity leave. Gabby's mother instigated a lifestyle for the family full of school, hobbies and socialising. Gabby's parents made time to assist with school and various activities, with the help of maternal grandparents who were direct neighbours and an influence on how the children were raised.

> Our childhood was so fast paced . . . [brother] was at footy, I was at ballet, [sister] was here, and [sister] was at swimming, it was like nana was looking after us, go to nana's, mum's working, like it was so, I don't remember much just like hanging at home like doing nothing . . . lots of fun, not so much routine, [or] structure.
>
> My nana was very, make sure us kids got opportunities and got to go out and do things and stuff . . . nana always said to my mum, 'send the kids to public schools so that they can—you can have money to go on holidays and do hobbies and extra things like that'. So we would do a lot.

"You always want to impress people and you always want to get better marks"

Gabby's family supported her ballet classes, especially her mother and grandmother, who also encouraged Gabby to wear feminised clothing. At ballet, Gabby received constant direction, compliments and criticism from the teachers, who taught her to monitor and control her body. If Gabby was able to create the right shape and movement, then she would receive performance opportunities and better grades on exams, allowing her to progress to another level.

> I remember being aware of my body and shape and weight because they'd say things like, 'where you sit you spread, long lean lines, gotta be light on your feet, waist in, ribs in, belly in'. . . . They weren't specifically like 'you're too fat'.

Secondary school

"I needed to keep this to myself because if people find out they might try and stop me"

Gabby sought weight-loss strategies from the ballet industry, her ballet community, family and friends, media like magazines and biographies about eating disorders. Gabby's fat-phobia was removed from mainstream feminine beauty standards, but her ballerina body received positive attention from people across her life.

> At school, one guy said that I was really hot but I was too skinny . . . never focus on that he thinks I'm hot, like here's an older guy, it was just like I'm stoked that he

thought I was too skinny. . . . I actually didn't care that I didn't look like a woman or becoming a woman or whatever.

> *I was obsessed with ballet companies and what they looked like . . . because I was so like into my ballet and a lot of people—family, friends—'Oh she does ballet, she's a ballerina, pretty ballerina'. People just, I felt like that kind of became my identity a bit, in my head I was like 'slim, skinny, ballerina, light'.*

"We didn't get pizza treats or anything like that"

Meals at home were monitored by her mother to ensure they were "healthy", and Gabby was always aware of her mother's own dieting, but as Gabby got older she would join her mother in dieting, exercise and talk about food and bodies and a way of interacting.

> *[Mum] she's very harsh on herself. Like when she says that she's got 'no control' I think she's, it's an exaggeration . . . mum's tiny, she's never been overweight . . . she does talk very negatively about herself, not to everyone, but at home.*
>
> *She talked to me about it, oh she was younger, if she had to lose weight for something, she would just live off coffee and cigarettes and an apple a day. And so then I was getting all these ideas.*

"I remember still thinking like 'oh no, it can't be anything mental'"

Entering secondary school, Gabby experienced a racing heart and could not sleep because she was worrying about her performance at school and ballet. Gabby's mother took her to the doctors and they left with an anxiety pamphlet. Her mother spoke to teachers so that they might support her at school, but otherwise there was little response.

> *He gave us a pamphlet for anxiety . . . she didn't do anything more with that, I was embarrassed, and she was shocked, and she didn't know how to fix that, so she just kind of shoved it away.*
>
> *Mum had to speak to the teachers at school, and they were just trying to help me but I was just like, that freaked me out, I was like, 'what are they trying to help with? Nope, nothing's wrong with me, I just need to do my best and focus'.*

"It can be hard to bring certain things up"

The family would exchange acts of service and spend quality time together, but conversations were dominated by light-hearted banter, and serious emotions were not given attention or were dismissed.

> *We all love each other, but we're not like lovey dovey. I've never seen my parents say they love each other, never seen them hold hands . . . mum never hugs me, dad never hugs me, they never say they love me.*

A lot of humour in our house . . . which is really good because it is funny, a lot of funny stuff, but then it's like, if I want to be serious, it's so hard to be serious.

Their generation age and stuff, they were kind of like, 'get on with it, harden the fuck up' . . . that's why my parents drink . . . it comes out in different ways . . . they don't know how to deal with serious emotions.

"Being that middle child, I didn't get left out, not at all, but I think they just thought that I would always be alright"

Gabby got messages from her parents that she was "keeping the family together" so when increasing demands from home, school and ballet threatened her "golden child" reputation, she silently worked harder and avoided burdening her parents. Her parents had become preoccupied with disciplining her older brother and helping her younger sister, leaving little attention for Gabby. Being the eldest daughter, Gabby also took on a caring role with her sister.

Mum and dad were more focused on him [brother] because he was not doing his homework, drinking, drugs . . . I think I just naturally did it [helped sister] a bit. My brother just was like, 'eh, whatever' . . . she [sister] would kind of want to hang out with me more.

"I wanted to be a ballerina, and that's what was gonna happen, and I had to make sacrifices, and this is just what I had to do"

Following a rejection from the national ballet school at age 13, Gabby was determined to work hard and optimise her strengths to succeed *as a ballerina*, in something outside the family of course. Half-way through secondary school, her ballet teacher helped her win a scholarship to a private all-girls school that would accommodate her training schedule.

I had a lot of the physical things there anatomically, not perfect, but . . . if I don't have the perfect this, the perfect that, then I'm gonna work really hard to at other things and change my body to be the best it has to be for me.

Older girls in ballet, some of them were leaving school and doing school online or over the phone and going to ballet full time.

"It was just this intense period of money issues and fighting in the family, that just never happened"

Gabby's parents were experiencing financial stress, drinking more and getting into arguments. On one occasion, when Gabby got involved in her parents fighting, her father became uncharacteristically violent towards her. Gabby avoided home and her father by picking up extra ballet classes.

I love my dad, but he did hit me once, and he has punched a hole through my door, and threw hot coffee at me. . . . I could have said something quite rude or shocking that I probably hadn't said to them before, I dunno, like 'shut the fuck up' . . . and you don't know how to react afterwards because it's, this isn't something that happens all the time.

I messaged a friend, who he [dad] didn't know that friend . . . I didn't want them to be that close to me. But they, she was like, 'you can come round here if you need'. So I knew that, I wasn't driving, I didn't have a car . . . I literally stayed up all night.

"They basically said all lots of teenage girls go through this, and I was discharged with little follow up"

Gabby started lying to her parents and staying home from school and ballet. On advice from teachers, Gabby went to a psychologist, but she did not talk to them about her eating disorder or her thoughts of suicide. After a near suicide attempt Gabby ended up in the hospital.

Started seeing this psychologist who I just did not click with . . . she would just give me homework to do and like 'I'm not fucking doing homework, I wanna kill myself'.

Mum was on night duty so she was in bed and I just walked into her room and said, 'mum, I tried, I nearly [suicided], I want to kill myself'. And she hadn't known it was that bad at the time. So she called my doctor and my psychologist and I actually got admitted.

There was a girl in there with an eating disorder . . . I remember being like, 'Oh my god, I can't tell anyone that I have problems with food or I'll end up in hospital'. So I remember being like, 'I have to be so secretive'.

"I was like 'yes, this is all happening, I can move away, out of home' and there was stressful things at home as well happening"

Gabby completed school remotely and worked part time, where she met new people including a boyfriend, and she avoided her parents further by staying at his house. After a six-month break, Gabby returned to dance slowly and the ambition to become a ballerina returned. She got accepted into a prestigious academy interstate and relocated.

That was happy for me because I could just do school from home, go to work, make money, meet new friends and do my own thing. And I didn't want to do anything else. And then I started to get a bit better.

It wasn't just me going, 'oh I'm gonna go run away to on the circus'. . . . I got into [the academy] which is a small amount of people getting in the first place, and then I've been doing it my whole life and then obviously my teachers . . . they encouraged it as well. . . . I did apply for uni and stuff at the same time just in case I changed my mind or didn't, so yeah [parents] they were completely supportive.

Ballet academy

"The career is not long, so it's why everything is so condensed, that's why it's very full on"

During her years at the academy, Gabby's strategies for losing weight varied and often depended on what the people around her were doing themselves or encouraging. Gabby had periods of depression after either using up all her energy reserves, or in response to "not doing well" when she did eat and put on weight. Gabby competed all three years of her degree, with some time off in-between, but each year her capacity to cope reduced further.

> *I got so many compliments and I got better roles and it was just like, everything seemed like it was happening because I was losing weight . . . then I was suddenly not getting roles and then getting depressed . . . there was all this pressure . . . having to try to go to classes every day and see my body in the mirror, and I was so embarrassed and ashamed, I felt numb. . . . I just wanted that like, to go away and come back and be like, have everyone think 'that's better, she's ready now, she looks good'. . . . For like a split moment I actually saw how skinny I was and I was like 'omg', I actually felt a bit grossed out by it, and then he [teacher] said 'but it's fabulous', and then I was 'eh okay'.*

"There's not a lot of jobs, but if you have the determination, commitment and skill, there is work for you"

The ballet industry provided a short career and limited opportunities for stable work. At Gabby's academy, she trained alongside a cohort of 12 students and only one would be selected for the company. The students competed for performance roles and the attention of directors who would scout talent.

> *Directors coming in and watching classes and picking out people . . . if the director comes in and sees us in class, at the bar, he's going to go around and look at who has the right body. . . . We were told he likes pretty, thin girls, with good feet.*

"They had the power, and they knew everyone so you would kind of do anything to do what they say because you feel like they're going to help you"

Gabby followed the directions of those who might help her access to career opportunities—choreographers, teachers, directors and students. The staff objectified the students, encouraged weight-loss strategies and prevented the students from seeking support for their eating disorders.

> *They would control us as much to be like . . . if we were on the pill, what pill we had to go on because there are certain pills that can make you gain weight and 'the company dances and on this one' . . . if you got sick and got a stomach flu, I remember*

the teacher being like 'oh good way to lose a couple of kilos before a show, everyone try and catch it now'.

The dietician came in as a group to speak to everyone about healthy eating and she specialised in eating disorders, and we all thought it was the most hilarious thing ever. We were just like, 'We're ballerinas, we live off water, a coffee—black coffee, and a piece of chocolate when we're about to faint, and we drink, and we smoke, so' and we just laughed at it.

A part of me that wanted help because I knew how exhausted I was . . . and I remember my head ballet teacher just saying to me, 'oh we will keep this between you and I, we won't tell the head of the school' because she would make me go get help.

"I still felt like it was okay at that time for that to happen because I think just growing up in this—in that place where men, you just do what they want"

During one of the academy parties, Gabby was sexually assaulted by an older male actor. Later at the academy he apologised to her, but Gabby felt like it was her fault somehow, so she told him not to worry about it. The sexual assault paralleled her experience in the classroom, where some of the older male choreographers sexualised the young dancers from their position of power.

He was older, so he was about 10 years older . . . it definitely planted seeds of like, okay, men are maybe a bit scary. . . . I felt like my body was just a bit of a, I dunno, a piece of play dough . . . at the time, no, it didn't affect me, just kind of, I put it in the box and put it away . . . but I think it's definitely had an influence on my relationships with men and being able to find a partner and feel safe.

Male dancers who are teaching you, and it's very sexualised, it doesn't seem like it would be, but it is . . . you're just thinking, 'oh I have to do this, I have to, he's that choreographer, or that teacher is liking me, so I have to'. Not anything like, not sexual assault, but just bordering on that inappropriate.

"Her trying to control the situation and my mum is very controlling . . . I was going through things but also growing up more and we just clashed"

Gabby's mother did not understand what was going on with her daughter, and her frustrations and efforts to "fix" Gabby resulted in conflict between them. Gabby's maternal auntie invited Gabby to travel back home with her to get respite from the tension.

Mum would make me feel guilty, bad for feeling bad, and she didn't understand . . . everyday she would just be like 'get up and go do and blah' and she would just 'nag nag nag'. . . . She was worried and concerned and anxious and when she's like that it's like, she literally turns into a crazy person, and just wants to fix everything, but also complain about everything, and she can't sleep and she can't, she can't just listen.

> *I needed soft support around me, and I wasn't getting that at home, . . . and I just needed to get almost to that worse place that I just needed to be left alone for a while.*

"I ate and ate and ate because I was like, 'no one can see me out here, I'm in the country'"

Compared to Gabby's mother, her aunt communicated with affection, had no expectations and ate freely. Living rurally interstate meant there was no one to observe Gabby eat and put on weight. After six months of eating and resting, Gabby's depression ceased, but she used her new found energy to train for her final year at the academy.

> *There wasn't any 'we're not eating, we're not eating that', which at my home it's more, my mum's always trying to lose weight, so this is flip, total opposite. . . . [Auntie] she always had food around and she always made rich meals, and I didn't do anything for six months or something. . . . I look after their property and animals and stuff . . . had no pressure and just helped them . . . they gave me a lot of freedom.*
> *It wasn't the healthiest way to get things, but it allowed me to just 'be' and let the depression kind of ride its course . . . looking back, I wish I had gotten help through it, but I did come out of it, and then moved back.*

"I was doing some unhealthy things, and I think they definitely affected my mind"

Gabby resumed her final year in the cohort below, but remained friends with some previous peers, one now working in the company. She felt supported by her friends, but they partied often and used substances to pick themselves up, calm themselves down and lose weight.

> *I was just, I don't know, having fun, slash, some drugs help with weight-loss . . . that was just like, 'oh, this is so good, I don't even have to exercise more, or eat . . . not even hungry when I do that' and yeah so . . . my mind lost it and I pretty much had a manic—my first manic episode, and so leading up to that, no sleeping, no eating.*

"The psychiatrist said, this is going to be a long journey, it could take up to 10 years to get medication or anything like that right"

While presenting to the hospital for erratic and unusual behaviour, Gabby was detained under the Mental Health Act for being a risk to herself. She returned to her home state with a diagnosis of bipolar and anorexia nervosa and continued to receive psychiatric treatment.

> *I thought I was dying of cancer or a disease or something . . . and I wanted to die gracefully . . . I remember it in flashes, I woke up and my mum and my mum's best*

friend were at the end of the bed, and I just remember being like 'oh my god, I'm not dying'.

Life after the academy

"The eating disorder was there even though I didn't need it to be, to help me get a skinny body, to be a ballerina"

Gabby finished her studies at a school without the focus on ballet, but she continued to audition for dance opportunities. Gabby was not unwell during this period, but she was still trying to meet the expectations of auditions, jobs and people in her personal life.

> *It took a long time to accept that I'm not going to be a ballerina. . . . I got unwell and I wasn't able to go back to dance and I was getting older. . . . I get so sad and my mum gets so sad as well because . . . she'd come over to see my shows and she'd just be blown away with how much I've improved and how good I was.*
>
> *It still was my identity to be a slim dancer, because that's what all my friends, like they go 'oh [Gabby], she's dancer' or people like family-friends 'oh, she's beautiful Gabby, she looks like a ballerina' . . . so there's part of me that sometimes still feels like I have to keep up that . . . I just want to be anonymous, I don't want to have that attached to me all the time and I feel like it is . . . I just want to be '[Gabby]'.*

"You're not in it [ballet] for the money, you're not in it for consistent work, and it's the passion, and the lifestyle, and the people you meet"

Event service and fitness instructing were considered interim jobs by Gabby who wanted a "passion" career. When Gabby discovered a novel course in movement therapy, she quickly relocated interstate to do the one-year course.

> *In this transition stage of 'well, I've got a job, I'll just save some money and I'm not sure what I'm gonna do . . . then I found out about this course, movement therapy, and I was just like 'oh my god, that would actually be amazing'. . . . The lady that ran the course was amazing, she's won some award from the queen . . . done PhDs . . . incredible women who have just dedicated their lives to dance and movement and healing . . . [Mum] she was just blown away by everyone there and the teachers.*

"I just started to have that like 'I need to get better' . . . I was feeling anxious about the next year"

Gabby had a full life, working two jobs, studying, renting a shared house, meeting new people and socialising. Pressure built towards the end of the year with submitting assignments, family visiting for graduation, lease coming to an end and promoting herself in a niche marketplace.

I was studying movement therapy, but I hadn't thought much beyond that. . . . I wasn't confident enough to go out there and find work or volunteer or do this and I just wanted something in the area. . . . I didn't want to fall into just working and living [interstate] even though that's fine, but I wanted to do something in what I was interested in.

"It felt like a bit of a Band-Aid fix, and I got quite depressed after"

In therapy, little time was spent exploring Gabby's life outside of the eating disorder. Shortly after graduation, Gabby's psychiatrist admitted her into a private eating disorder ward for two months.

[Psychiatrist] she would never ask just, 'how are you going, what are your plans for next year?' . . . She really didn't help me and give me that just extra bit of confidence from someone else saying, 'things will be okay, there's options, there's other things we can do, don't lose it' like when I needed it, if I was feeling anxious or depressed.

Suddenly thrown into a room with a bunch of other women or men that have various types of eating disorders . . . the sick part of you is like 'I need to be the thinnest here . . . got to do it right one more time, get to that really low weight', and it kind of started to consume me even when I was in hospital and even though I was eating more.

"I kind of felt like a failure that I had to come back"

Retreating to her family home allowed Gabby to rest and focus on recovery, but not working or studying evoked guilt around wasting her privilege and potential. Gabby cycled between episodes of depression and disordered eating. She received electro-convulsive therapy (ECT), medication reviews, therapy and other admissions to hospital.

Here I am, an abled body, young person . . . I couldn't work to make money, I felt guilty that I wasn't contributing to society. . . . I took up space and I was just annoying and a burden to everyone, and I felt selfish for feeling that way too because I'm lucky with everything.

"You have to get to a certain point to think you're even valid enough to get the help you deserve"

The eating disorder provided purpose, something to live for, and kept the thoughts of suicide at bay. But the eating disorder also received greater attention from people, which helped her feel "sick enough" to deserve support.

The guilt and shame I felt with the depression, when I was unwell and admitted to the eating disorder ward, I didn't have the guilt and shame as much because it was like, 'oh well, I look unwell' and these people are coming to see me and they're now, they're saying, 'oh my god, thank god you're here'.

More feedback that Gabby was "sick enough" came when she barely got the medical clearance to travel overseas for a wedding. It was a wake-up call for Gabby to be outside of her comfort zone without the safety net of her treatment team. She agreed to admit to the eating disorder ward on her return.

> *Because there's a part of you, and people are lying if they don't own up to that, but there's a part of you that wants someone to step in and take over and take all the control away, because you're in so much pain physically and emotionally.*

Recovery

"There's no quick fix, and it's hard work, and it's constant, and it's everyday making good decisions"

Gabby understood recovery to be an ongoing journey with daily self-monitoring to make the right choices. Gabby's recovery was defined by stable eating and mood, and the desire to be well. She still had fat-phobic thoughts, and for Gabby weighing herself permitted her to eat with reassurance that she was not getting too big.

> *My doctor was talking about this the other day, even now that I'm in a good place, I'm still very, very vulnerable, because the pull to go back, and then you start just doing a few little things, then it can just like yeah, very, gotta keep on top of it.*
>
> *I don't feel comfortable in my body but I'm learning . . . I do worry about people . . . not so much strangers, more people I know, friends, families, and cause I know people think it, like friends and family . . . some family that we might only see at big events . . . when I've been at a bit heavier stage people just don't comment at all, I'm like what gives you permission to comment on me when I'm underweight and unhealthy yet if I'm fat . . . it would be really hard for my mum because she wouldn't want to like upset me, but I feel like it would be really hard for me if I gained more weight . . . I associate being fat with being lazy and being like, you haven't got any control, and you're not doing well. . . . When people see me like that, it's like in their head they're like . . . 'she's let herself go'. . . . If I was at the beach and a very obese man or woman walk past, I'd probably in my head go, 'oh my gosh, they're so overweight' or same with a really skinny person.*

"The guilt's gone because I've finally realised that this isn't me, this isn't my fault, I didn't ask for any of this, but I'm a good person, and I can do it"

More than medication and talking about eating and body-image, Gabby's psychiatrist helped her gain more influence in her relationships. The psychiatrist gave Gabby permission to not be okay in a way that her family had not previously offered.

> *My doctor was like 'if you get up and have a shower, that's amazing, if you get up and get to the couch, that's amazing' . . . my doctor wouldn't even entertain the idea*

of doing something like work or study . . . she'd have to tell me, 'no you are unwell'. It's taken me a long time to accept that those things, they are an illness and they're not a choice . . . I like seeing my doctor, I'm not embarrassed, I'm not ashamed about things . . . if anything I feel really proud of myself that I've overcome that all these things in my life and just like someone with cancer or just like someone with diabetes or autism or whatever.

"I could probably say the exact same thing as my doctor, but because it's coming from my doctor, it's like my mum and my dad can listen and actually take it seriously"

Gabby's psychiatrist helped her gain influence in the family by coaching Gabby in conversations, in session mediation, providing parenting advice over the phone and referring her parents to a support group.

> *Down the track, I have gotten them [parents] to come into my appointments, and my doctor has spoken to them, and my doctor will call my mum . . . she can hear it better from professional as opposed to me . . . if it was me doing it then I feel like I just get yelled at or not listen to but when it's through someone else . . . you feel listened to, you feel validated.*
>
> *Mum actually went to a parent's group . . . I think that was the best thing she could have done because they, she said at the beginning 'this is lame' and they had to do like roleplay and stuff, but my dad went too, and it's been so much better since then, so much.*

"We don't do any of that stuff together anymore . . . the things we do together more now are just healthier things, like she's going to teach me how to knit"

It was advised that Gabby's mother no longer share conversations or activities about weight-loss, and build a new relationship with food by preparing meals together and consistently offering Gabby food.

> *I do want people to offer me food, because it's like I feel like I can't ask for it because then I feel guilty . . . people with eating disorders want, they're screaming out for help and begging you to just offer them some food. It's almost like if you don't do it, then it's kind of enabling them.*
>
> *Sometimes I just want to know if I'm fat or not, and I feel like I can't ask anyone but her [mum], I just want an honest answer and she won't even engage in it with me. . . . She still wants to lose weight, but she doesn't talk to me about numbers or weight. . . . She doesn't mean to, but she complains about her weight and she will get diet books out, but she tries to keep it to herself more.*

"My brother had his baby, his first baby, and I just did it, I just starting eating at home"

The family dynamics changed with births and deaths that opened up new roles for people. Gabby had never considered having children until she observed her brother as a father and her parents as grandparents. It helped Gabby imagine a new future for herself, one that was not compatible with the eating disorder.

I could see how happy my mum and my dad were and it's just brought this whole new layer to our family . . . brought so much joy . . . first time I think I ever actually thought, 'I want children', so that was a huge thing that has helped me a lot. Used to be when I was younger . . . I've got to do like the biggest things and I've got to be, do amazing things, but I think as things have progressed and changed and experiences and family and I've gone, I don't need to save the world or become a famous whatever . . . if I had a little job, family—stoked.

It [recovery] came with a real sense of I want a life, you have to want a life more than you want the eating disorder. And I want to find someone, I want to have a family, I want a job, I want to buy my own house . . . if I have children, one, I have to be healthy to do it, I have to have a partner, I don't have to, but I would like to have a partner to do it with . . . I can't imagine myself being fat and happy unless I was pregnant, maybe.

"I talk to my doctor about all of these things, and she acknowledges the person I am, she reminds me what I've done, what I've accomplished"

Gabby took on caring roles for her nephews and her late maternal grandmother, which allowed her to demonstrate and be acknowledged for her strengths. Gabby developed her non–ballerina and non–eating disorder identity by drawing on her experiences of caring, studying movement therapy and working as a teacher.

I was pretty much her [grandmother's] carer, not officially, but I'd go around every day and I would help her. . . . I'm really good working with the elderly and children, and not everyone is in those areas, or it might be hard for them, when it comes quite naturally to me. . . . There is a lot more to me than what people might see, and my mum is actually very good and she is starting to see a lot more.

Teaching is actually, I think definitely something that makes me feel better . . . you don't realise how much knowledge you have from your dance and body and this, until you get in there and you have to teach. . . . I actually found that job really kind of empowering . . . it wasn't about me, it's about them. . . . I wanted them to come in and enjoy the class and just leave feeling like they've been looked after.

I don't identify as a dancer anymore . . . not in the way people think dancing should be that make sense . . . movement will always be a part of my life in one way or another. . . . I'm so curious about the body and the mind and movement and those sort of things. That's what I feel like I'm more about now. . . . I'm using what I've learned then to do what I want to do.

"[The psychiatrist] she's been really a big supporter of me, moving out and finding a place of my own"

Although Gabby had more influence with her parents, some of the same issues continued, and Gabby had plans to move out so the relationship could be more on her own terms.

> [Mum] she always wants to know everyone's business . . . only because she wants the best for people, but she just has to let go and realise that we all have to make up our own minds and do things in our own time.
>
> Now that I am well, I think that my mum is just like 'get a job'. . . . I'm literally about to get another job but like a supermarket just to tie me over and move out of home. . . . I 100% think that my relationship with my parents and my family will be so much better when I moved out because it's just, it's too much, living together in the same household.

7 Diane's story

Sisters and solitude

Diane's childhood was characterised by restriction. Restriction about who she could play with, what she could believe and what she should eat. Moving continents and sharing a small bedroom with her three sisters further limited her opportunities for autonomy. Diane controlled the few elements of her life that she could. The start of her exercise obsession overlapped with her mother suggesting they start a diet together. Ten years later while living out of home and studying acting, Diane had exposure to different contexts and relationships that aided her recovery. Although she has considered herself recovered for four years, Diane speaks about some of the struggles she still has with body-image, eating and exercise.

Childhood

The earliest story Diane told about her body was her mother's comments about her belly being round. Although this was not described as being inherently negative, Diane ascribed meaning to what her mother was saying.

> I kind of kept my baby fat for a while, but I've always had just a little stomach, a little peach. My mum used to rub it all the time. She called it my 'buddha belly'. I never lost it throughout childhood. So even when I was around 11, my mum would always rub my belly, my buddha belly. She probably thought it was so harmless, that it was so cute. But eventually it became, 'Wait, I don't like that'. And I think I was super aware of not liking this physical part of my body.

Diane was hyper aware of the perceived discrepancy between herself and her sisters' beauty. Being "less beautiful" than her sisters did not bother her when she was a young tomboy, but there were seedlings of insecurity and comparison from an early age.

> I've got three really beautiful sisters. And I always felt like I was the ugly duckling. I have really big teeth and a massive overbite. And I just felt I was, yeah, less pretty. . . . I didn't really care when I was much younger, I was quite a tomboy. Most of my best friends were boys. And we lived next to a forest. So I spent a lot of my

DOI: 10.4324/9781003453918-9

childhood just playing in the woods. And so it was, it was a really great childhood.
I don't remember, I can't remember having any feelings of insecurities about how
I looked or anything. But I know I always sort of had that in the back of my mind.

Diane was particularly observant of her oldest sister's beauty, comparing her
body to her sister's long figure in ballet, despite her sister being nearly two years
older. Being enrolled in ballet for a period in childhood did not bring about any
eating or body behaviours, but Diane did experience discomfort in her body
being on display.

> *I definitely noticed that my older sister was very beautiful. I started ballet a little bit*
> *in the States before we moved. I think probably from the ages of around 8 to 10. . . .*
> *My sister was doing it as well, and she far more had the physicality of a ballerina.*
> *Very long legged, very lean. I say all of these things now because I can look back and*
> *I can see that, but I don't think it was anything super conscious in my head. . . . I*
> *don't think I was super concerned about how I looked or anything. But I remember*
> *feeling awkward. . . . You're wearing a random leotard and you're around a bunch*
> *of mirrors all the time. It wasn't anything that serious, it was probably completely*
> *normal, but I think it was just planting seeds.*

Diane's family lived in a semi-rural area of the United States. They were very
religious, and Diane was not allowed to socialise outside of their religious community. She was the second eldest of four sisters, with a six-year age range
between them, and they were exclusively home-schooled by their mother. Her
parents closely monitored the sister's behaviour, only permitting them to attend
some extra-curricular activities, and the sisters were often enrolled in the same
team or class.

> *I was home-schooled, home-schooled all the way through, from year one, from pre-*
> *school or kindergarten or whatever, until year 12. So all of my sisters were, my*
> *parents decided to do that, because I had a couple of family friends who were home-*
> *schooled and they just decided to do that.*
> *My dad worked and my mum stayed home with all of my sisters and I. They*
> *decided to do it because they had friends who home-schooled and they wanted to give*
> *it a go. And I don't think they were very happy with the schools around the area*
> *anyway. Was also sort of a money saving thing. My family has never been particu-*
> *larly wealthy, we really haven't had a lot of money, and we saved a lot of money by*
> *home-schooling.*

Diane mostly enjoyed having sisters of a similar age and sharing friends. Most
of their peers had similar restrictions because they were known through their
parents' religious community and were also home-schooled. So Diane was not
bothered by many of these restrictions, as it was all she knew. Diane equated
obedience and compliance with praise. She would never lie or disobey her parents and was always a good Christian daughter. Diane described all of her sisters

as good and perfect in their own ways, seeing them as each having their own area they excelled in or were recognised for.

> *I was a very good child. I would never lie. I never went out without telling my parents where I was or anything.*

Diane attributed the development of her temperament, introversion, to having less opportunity to socialise with a range of people in her youth. She had some concerns about her ability to recognise and adopt socially normative behaviour in groups, but also saw the benefit in not getting caught up in a popularity contest.

> *Not being around that constant social atmosphere, sometimes I do struggle sometimes in social situations. That makes me question myself and not knowing what the general social atmosphere is. Sometimes it's good, though, because I just usually don't care. So in big social groups, I'm not really worried about impressing whoever was top dog, or being part of a certain group or something. . . . I would experience some of it in whatever clubs I was in. I would think, 'Oh, there is a separate group over there, and everyone wants to be in that group, but I don't really get why'. I was always a floater. I didn't really think, 'The popular group is this group'. I was just kind of in every group, because I wasn't aware that there was the kind of delineation. Which has been a good thing and a bad thing.*

Diane was grateful to be home-schooled, where she did not have to compete with other students, could focus on her studies and work independently.

> *I'm personally very grateful that I was home-schooled . . . because I'm quiet, I like studying, I really do really like learning. And I think because I was introverted, I think if I'd been in a school context, I would have really struggled to focus because sometimes if I'm in a social situation, I really find it hard to focus. I need to be in my little bubble and my shell. And so not having those kind of social distractions, I was able to really focus on my studies, and I'm a good student.*
>
> *I was very, I think it was very quite privileged, actually, with the education that I had. Because there was only four students in my class. And obviously, I was in a different year levels of the rest of the students.*
>
> *By the time I was in year 11 and 12, my education was pretty self-led. So it was quite similar to I guess university, where you're pretty self-motivated and you have to guide yourself through all of it. . . . My mum would check my tests and things and check in on me sometimes, but a lot of times it would just be me.*

Move to Australia

Diane's childhood was disrupted when she was 10 years old and her family moved to Australia from the United States. Her mother's family lived in Australia, and they chose to uproot their lives and move to be close with them.

However, moving countries led to many challenges. Her father's struggle to secure stable employment was a barrier to settling in a new country, because her mother had to find work for the first time, and the family moved in with maternal relatives, which provided little space or privacy.

> *And then we moved. So we moved to Australia when I was 10. Which was a big thing, obviously very life changing. Scary. But I'm pretty good at adapting quickly. I remember it was really hard for my family when we moved here. My dad had a job in the States and he is very artistic and very experienced, and he could pretty easily pick up a job in the States. But when we moved here, none of those things mattered anymore. And I mean, he really struggled to find work. He went through so many different jobs and was really struggling to support a family, and my mum started working for the first time ever to support us as well. And it was a struggle.*
>
> *We lived in my grandma's very, very small two-bedroom apartment for a family of six. So we were all sharing a room and I think mum and dad slept in the living room . . . I've shared a room throughout my whole life, until I moved out this year.*

The overseas relocation was more difficult for Diane compared to her sisters, who were more extroverted and made friends easier. Her parents' financial instability meant that extra-curricular activities were limited, but Diane was enrolled into acting classes without her sisters, and this helped her to develop friendship-making abilities.

> *Since I was less of a social creature, I didn't really make a bunch of friends when I first got here or anything.*
>
> *I remember right before we left the States we went to see a lot of our friends in school plays. I've never particularly been interested in drama before then, but I saw them and I was like, 'Oh my goodness. I want to do this'. So as soon as we got here, I said, 'Mum, I want to join a drama club'. She found me some local classes within the first four or five months of us being here.*

The family continued to home-school in Australia. Spending a majority of her time with her siblings and mother, Diane was exposed to similar rhetoric with little opportunity to challenge them or be exposed to disconfirming evidence. The discourse relating to food and bodies framed 'overweight' as disorderly and normalised weight-loss behaviours as healthy.

> *I've noticed habits of my mum, of her, just little things like when you eat, when I eat a piece of cake or something being like, 'This is just a treat', or, 'Oh, this is so naughty'. That language around food.*
>
> *She'd say, 'I'm doing this thing, I'm finally going to get myself in order'. As if she was always out of order. But she's always looked after herself and eaten well, and she's really active but she's never been happy with her body . . . she always talks about it as if it's a 'health thing'.*
>
> *My mum often talked about losing weight. . . . It was just kind of a running theme. It was never, 'I'm going on a diet', or, 'I'm trying to lose weight', or, 'I'm so fat'. It wasn't anything like that, it was just the discrete dialogue around it.*

She had four children. And she breastfed all of us, except for my last sister. Now she always says she wishes she had because she breastfed to lose the baby weight. She didn't breastfeed my last sister, so she feels like she never lost the baby weight.

Due to Diane's limited social circle, she would often accompany her older sister to social activities. When Diane joined her sister at a gym class for the first time, she felt weak and inadequate, and did not return to avoid exercising in the audience of others. But she continued to exercise at home around her family, and to progress her strength and fitness.

I think I was probably around 12 or 13, maybe. And my sister was going to our local gym. There were youth classes that they did three or four times a week or something. And it was just a personal trainer who would just lead teenagers through a workout or something. And she was going to that because a friend of hers was, and one time I went along with her. And I did this class. And it was super fun. I've never worked out before or done any exercise in that way. We did boxing, and lifting weights, things like that. And it was really fun. But I've always been quite a small person and not particularly strong. And I was the youngest in the class. And I felt 'so' weak. And the personal trainer was also really attractive. And I was like, 'I'm never going back'. I felt quite uncomfortable and so self-conscious about that. And I thought, 'Yeah, I'm never going back'. But I enjoyed exercising. So I was like, 'Well, I'll just do it on my own'. So I started exercising on my own at home, sometimes out in the living room while my mum's cooking dinner or something, and I'd say, 'Look! I can do push-ups now!'

Diane took up her exercise routines at home around the same time that her mother invited her on an eight-week diet. The diet was an opportunity to be close to her mother through shared practice. Her mother encouraged restrictive eating because she said that it exhibited a level of discipline. Diane admitted that she thrived on this validation from her mother and sought it out whenever possible.

I think the discovery of exercise also overlapped with when my mother and I quit sugar together . . . you cut out every kind of sugar . . . I know now this isn't sustainable. Fruit is very important, but they just want to readjust your palate . . . at the end of it, you start bringing back in fruit and things like that.

It did make me hyper-conscious of food and the things I was eating. . . . It didn't begin with a super obsessive, 'I care about everything I eat', but it just made me very aware. . . . Looking at nutrition labels and stuff . . . then eventually it becomes, 'What is this exact ingredient?' and, 'If it's got this ingredient, then it's bad'. Being very black and white.

I was pretty annoying during that stage of life because I would be pretty judgmental of other people's food. I would make comments if I saw something, 'Well, did you know that's actually got whatever in it?' Eventually I learned that that was pretty unkind.

My mum has said, 'You have really good self-control, because of what you've done'.

Development of eating disorder

It was not long until Diane was no longer dieting and exercising for her mother's approval, but for reasons she could not articulate, only abstract ideas like 'control' and 'focus'. She recognised that the amount of physical activity she was doing was no longer being praised, and she resorted to maintaining secrecy of her habits to avoid comments from her family. This opposed her "good daughter" role, and Diane was worried about damaging the relationship between her and her parents.

> *I'm a perfectionist, and I was doing everything perfectly. So, I had to do this perfectly, too. . . . It wasn't so much, 'You need to lose weight' or 'need to be more beautiful', or something. There was far more focus around control.*
>
> *For the first time in my life, I was lying to my parents, which was probably one of the worst parts about it all. I do think it really sort of damaged my relationship with them.*
>
> *Every time I worked out, I always had to add a little bit more. So eventually, I got to the point where I was exercising in more than inordinate amounts. . . . I was being home-schooled, so I could be in any room of the house. Well, while I did school, I would usually try to keep as active as possible. I would hate sitting down. I would take walks throughout the day listening to audio recordings for a class. I would go for sprints. And then usually at the end of the day, I'd be like, 'I'm just going to stretch', or whatever. And I would do an intense yoga session. And it was all very secretive.*

Diane started to realise the ramifications of her behaviour gradually as she analysed some aspects of her functioning and social life that had changed since engaging in excessive exercise and restrictive eating.

> *I didn't really make many friends. Well, keep many friends. I was always a nice person and I wanted to be friends with people. But I really struggled because, I don't know . . . I know more now. It's not just, psychologically you're damaged . . . it really does affect you, not just physically but your brain. When you're underfed, you're not nourished, you can't think properly. And so now I've learned how much easier it is to think and feel properly when I'm eating enough, and I'm well rested. So I just didn't really interact very well with people because I was hungry all the time without even knowing it . . . the only emotion that I felt was anxiety. Because if my parents caught me exercising, or I was prevented from exercising when I wanted to, I would just get so anxious and on the verge of tears because I was so stressed out. . . . I thought, 'I can't keep living like this where I'm so delicate and sensitive'. . . . There were a number of 'Yes, it's time. I need to stop this'. But I think that was a slow burn. It was a realisation of 'I can't keep doing this'. . . . I was gripping white knuckled on to this specific structure I had when I worked out and when I ate and what I ate. And if one thing was slightly nudged it would just ruin my whole day.*

Towards recovery

Diane considered stopping her eating disorder behaviours when her friends and immediate family began to tell her of their concerns. It was not until her behaviour had become extreme and her appearance was drastically changed that people around her started to intervene.

> *Friends or relatives would see me, and they would just be so shocked or hurt. . . . I remember when my American grandma came and visited us. I think her visit was pretty coloured by the fact that she was so concerned for me and what was going on.*
>
> *It was mainly my relationship to other people that made me want to recover. And my parents really saying, 'This is bad'. I think they were quite afraid. And probably quite scared by what I was doing, what I was going to do, and I didn't really understand it. They knew it was bad. And I think I could see how much I was damaging my relationship with them. And also, how much it was just maddening for myself, my whole life is wrapped around that.*
>
> *My dad wasn't around a lot of [recovery]. My mum typically was very support-ive, but she didn't understand a lot. . . . I wasn't forced into anything. It really was self-motivated. . . . My parents had a strong hand in it in the way of 'no, you're going to sit down at the table with us and eat this meal', or, 'You're going to stop exercising'. But I could have kept doing it. I could have found ways to hide it. But I think I was just miserable. I realised how awful it was, and how I was just missing out on so much.*

While Diane was going through recovery, she also enrolled into acting school, as her hobby had grown into a potential career path. Despite going through recovery, Diane was still monitoring her food, restricting her eating and moving to lose weight. After using restrictive practices for so long, Diane struggled to find a balance with eating and exercising.

> *I had the reputation for being the health freak. I meal prepped everything, which was also a cost efficient thing, because I didn't really have the money to buy food out. But it was also a control thing. I would track my food and calories on an app, because I wanted to make sure I was eating. But I used that excuse but really, it was a control thing. So I would track all my meal prep and I wouldn't eat out whenever the group would go to eat out. And oftentimes, I would typically myself, every lunch break, going for a walk because I was stressed out because I was sitting for four hours in a class and I wasn't moving.*
>
> *But it was just the swing of the pendulum, I guess, from one extreme to the other. Sometimes I think I took it to an unhealthy strain for a period of the recovery there where I was like, 'Okay, I have to eat a lot. So, I'll just exercise a lot. And then I'll eat—I can eat whatever I want'.*

When Diane started acting school, her parents were experiencing conflict and money stress, but she did not talk much about this in the interview. Moving to a new country caused arguments between her parents, and Diane said that her parents fighting made her feel even more so that things were not in her control. There was uncertainty around if the family were going to go back to the States or not, and if her parents would divorce.

> *So I started acting school, just at the kind of beginning slash in the middle of my recovery. And also my parents' marriage was falling apart . . . things weren't working in their relationship anyway, it was probably inevitable. . . . I think it presented me with the opportunity to be like, I'm going back to my old habits. My control. . . .*

Going to acting school exposed Diane to a diversity of people, with diverse bodies and new discourses. Diane's acting school peers were exclusively women, many of which shared ideologies that contradicted those Diane had accepted as truth. Being exposed to many different women, Diane believed she was able to develop a more profound sense of what it means to be 'feminine' and the purpose of bodies.

> *That was probably one of the best things ever, doing drama. I still am an introvert, but I was a lot more introverted before I started doing drama. And before I was an introvert, and very uncomfortable. And I was like, 'Why? Why do I struggle to socialise?'*
>
> *Having a class of all women, but who all have very different bodies and who I think are all so beautiful. That really helps as well. Yes, probably the best situation really, I think it really helps my mental health. It's forced me to be around people for three to five days a week. So be out of my comfort zone in that way . . . be around people with very different body sizes. And also, you know, doing movement classes and just acting classes and learning new ways to express myself with my body.*

Through lessons in the social sphere of acting school, Diane identified that she was the type of person to "go with the flow" but needed some elements of control to feel grounded. She hypothesised that behaving in restrictive ways was her method of expressing control in an important, tangible area of her life.

> *My mum says all of our births reflect our personality. . . . My eldest sister was the super stubborn one, she was a very hard, painful birth. Apparently, I just slipped right out because I'm so chill.*
>
> *I always go with the flow. So I think the eating and the exercise was my way of, I go with the flow with everything else, this is the way I exert control. I usually go with the flow, because I have certain elements of control in my life that I rely on.*

Diane was previously restricted by rules of what she could or could not eat, which were informed by the messages she received from her mother at home. After acting in ways that contradicted these rules, she learnt there were no dreadful consequences.

I was just constantly proving to myself that these were things that I could do. I was like, 'Look, I can keep eating and I'm not gonna die'. And I've had so many moments of just breaking down the rules that I had for myself. Thinking, you can't eat that and do that. And I still have moments where I break rules that I didn't even realise I'd set for myself until I broke them.

So I remember a time where I ate three meals in a row, then I felt so uncomfortable in my body because I was so full and bloated. I was so stressed out and anxious because I took a nap in the middle of the day. After eating I didn't move until hours later. And I was so stressed when I woke up and realised, but at the same time I was also so determined. And I was like, 'I'm going to keep going'. So I woke up from my nap. And my dad, he's a really great cook, had just made a really nice meal. So, I ate that too and surprised myself, and the rest of the family too.

Going through treatment and recovery made Diane aware of the discourse of the family around eating and bodies that she had taken for granted. Diane never believed her sisters experienced the same challenges in relation to eating and body-image. Diane looked up to her older sister because of this, believing that she could exhibit greater self-control due to not being influenced or easily persuaded by the opinions of others.

I think because I became so aware of all the negative things I was doing, I became aware of all the negative things other people around me were doing as well. . . . When I was first going through recovery, I was super hypersensitive to language around food. I'd be like 'Mum, no, don't say that'. But now I think I can't do anything. But it would just always be like, 'Oh, this is good' or 'This is bad'. Or just always talking about what you're doing and what you've been eating like 'Oh, we went out to eat this and it was so indulgent, it was so crazy', Why can't it just be a thing? Just enjoy the taste of it.

Diane recognises that recovery is not linear, and that there may be many hurdles ahead in truly moving past her experiences with restrictive food and exercise practises. However, she has developed a more balanced relationship with her body and food, where she can appreciate the neutrality of having a body that serves a purpose.

Despite considering herself to be mostly recovered and well, Diane can acknowledge the persistence of some thoughts related to her body-image. Ultimately, she thinks back to being a little girl and her mother describing her stomach as a "Buddha belly" which Diane identifies as the first time she became aware of her body being anything but functional.

I still have this preoccupation with my stomach. Even when I was gaining back the weight, which happened pretty gradually. It wasn't all of a sudden, it was a slow process. But when you're so undernourished most of the time when you gain weight, it does go straight to your stomach, because that's where most of your organs are.

It's a protective thing. So I immediately noticed that, and I would hate touching my stomach. I would make sure my hands wouldn't touch my stomach because I hated feeling that it was coming back.

Diane still ruminates about the start of her poor relationship with food. Occasionally, she becomes frustrated or feels lost when attempting to figure out what triggered her eating disorder in the first place.

I'll never completely understand why it started. Maybe there was one thing that made it happen, or it was just a confluence of events, or it was always going to happen no matter the situation.

Although Diane experienced many restrictions on her behaviour because she was home-schooled, she understood her limited social sphere to be a protective context against the eating disorder being worse than it was, and her family to be her biggest supports towards recovery.

I don't know if I would have gone through the disordered eating habits that I did if I had been in school. Maybe it would have been worse, maybe I already had those inclinations in me. And if I had a bunch of other people to compare myself to and learn things from . . . I spent a lot of time talking to my parents and adults and all of my friends have all been around five years older than me most of the time. And I had older sisters around me, so I had people who might know more than me to help me and educate me. So that helped me get out of the habit. And I don't know what things might have been worse if I hadn't been home-schooled.

8   Bianca's story

Shrinking for love

Bianca's eating disorder was defined by a yearning for control and a fear of being negatively perceived. She received negative body-image messages from her extended family which were then reiterated to her when she was bullied in high school. The following quote summarises the perceived and real outcomes that served as the central catalyst for her eating disorder.

> *I thought that if I lost weight, then . . . everyone would love me. And that, I would have no problems in the world and that I would actually finally be pretty. Because I thought that being skinny and being pretty were completely correlated . . . I thought that . . . everyone would want to be my friend . . . no one would talk shit about me, and I'd get more Instagram followers, and . . . just everything that a contemporary woman would want, that's what I thought was going to happen. . . .*

Early life contexts

Immediate family

Bianca and her older brother were raised in a conservative, Catholic household. Their parents followed a "traditional" path in their relationship, a path they intended her to also follow.

> *He's a year older than her, she's a year younger. They met in uni. They dated for a year. They got engaged for a year, and then they were married. And then . . . three or four years later, they had two babies . . . it's the most traditional relationship ever . . . it was definitely expected that—yeah, I get married, have babies . . . it's that Catholic guilt. My nonna is still pushing for me to get married.*

Bianca's grandfather became a paraplegic around the time she was born and her father subsequently found himself in a carer role. Bianca's brother was also diagnosed with obsessive compulsive disorder (OCD) when she was a young

DOI: 10.4324/9781003453918-10

child, meaning they were often taking him to appointments and giving him the attention he needed for his treatment.

> *When [my brother] was a kid . . . he was in therapy for [OCD]. . . . They thought maybe it was autism, but it turned out definitely OCD. . . .*
> *I think there were definitely periods of my childhood where I thought that I wasn't receiving the attention that a child should be. But my, my nonno—my grandpa, he became a paraplegic when I was born. And so, my dad had to put in a lot of attention to him . . . like my dad would work from seven to seven. And then he would go to his parents' house, and he would care for his dad. And then he would come home. And that was like, our routine . . . the attention wasn't really focused on me during probably like some very crucial developmental stages. But I know that my mum gave as much—maybe even too much attention to both me and my brother to like, kind of offset the fact that my dad didn't have the time.*

Extended family

Bianca's heritage is Italian on her father's side and Anglo-Australian on her mother's side. With this came a rich mix of cultural influence on her understanding of the world and what her role within it is.

Food is the language of love: Bianca's Italian family used food as a way to express love. It was something that brought them together.

> *Food is a way of people showing their love. And so sometimes it's forced. Sometimes it's like, 'Oh, why aren't you eating? eat, eat, eat'.*

Love, it is what's outside that counts: Bianca's family on her mother's side were overt in their affirmations of beauty and thin-ideals. These standards became apparent to Bianca when she was 8 and she began to feel as though she needed to shrink to feel loved.

> *So my mum's sister, she had two daughters, and they were both really thin. And my mum has another sister—sister one, sister two—sister two has the two children. Sister one always used to like idolise sister two's daughters, and think that they were so pretty and give them better gifts. And I used to compare myself to them, because I always looked at them and thought, 'Wow, they are so pretty, like no wonder they get the better gifts than I do. Like, it's because they're pretty and they're skinny'. . . . That's the first time I can pinpoint thinking like, 'Okay, I'm bigger than my cousins, even though they're older than me. I'm bigger, and I need to shrink to feel that same love'.*

Teenage years

Bianca's teenage years shaped the way she understood her place within society through the behaviours of those around her both past and present.

Learning to be a woman through . . .

As Bianca entered puberty and her body began to become more 'womanly', she looked to those around her to learn how to navigate this new chapter in her life.

. . . *family*: While growing up, there was minimal talk about Bianca's body-image or presentation. However, there were comments about other women which Bianca understood as an indication of how women are perceived by society.

> *They'll make little comments . . . like, if my mum sees like a bigger person on screen, she'll go like, 'Oh, wow, that's a big person, isn't it?' and it's like, 'Maybe that's how people see me. . . .'*

This fear of being negatively perceived was solidified when an auntie on her paternal side commented on Bianca's appearance.

> *One of my aunties . . . when I was about 15 . . . she said, 'You're big boned. And you have tiny boobs'. And at that time, my boobs were like, quite large for my figure. Because I was very slight back then . . . I just couldn't believe it. . . . Like if my bones are wide . . . I can't do anything about that. . . . But like she obviously meant to call me fat . . . let me just say that.*

As these were the people who were supposed to love her, Bianca feared that everyone else in society was seeing something much worse.

> *. . . If my own family makes comments like that, then, what does everyone else see?*

. . . *the "male gaze"*: At the age of 14, Bianca also started to observe the "male gaze" when men started to cat-call her on the streets. Bianca had learned that male attention was something that women want, however, she could not help feeling uncomfortable.

> *It's kind of confusing, 'cause it's kind of like, 'Oh I'm getting attention'— which is something that I think women are told that we want—we want attention. And so, I was like, 'Oh I'm getting attention from males, that's a good thing, but I don't want them to be commenting on the way I look, so it's a bad thing. . . .'*

School life, you cannot leave your homelife at home

Bianca struggled to maintain a social life with her peers throughout her high school years.

At home, her parents had strict rules, dictating the circumstances in which she could be social outside of school hours.

> *It's like, 'You can only have one social event a week. And you can't be out too late and you can't, you know, go for many sleepovers. And we need to know the parents before you can hang out'.*

This made it difficult to fit in with the other kids at school as, when Bianca began to fall victim to bullying, she was unable to mitigate the situation through additional social interactions.

> *I was really heavily bullied throughout high school . . . any little thing that you think a girl could be insecure about, they made me feel bad for and it's all because I think one girl didn't like me. And it just started like a chain reaction of like all the girls not liking me and they all convinced the boys not to like me. . . .*

This bullying further shaped Bianca's insecurities surrounding her body-image as being a determinant for worth, as well as her idea that men are socially expected to comment on women's bodies.

> *I was definitely aware of my body in high school . . . I just wanted to be . . . skinny and loved.*
>
> *This girl who . . . I was friends with her at one point, but then she ended up being one of the girls who bullied me. She had like, 0% body fat . . . she, like, hit her stomach. And then she hit mine. And she goes, 'Ours make such a different noise'. I was probably 13. And I think that's when the body-image like fixation on my stomach—that's like the predisposing like—that was one of the moments . . . obviously, men always comment on your body. That's just something that we have to deal with as a society, . . . but when it comes from a woman, knowing that most women have that universal struggle, it hurts a lot more.*

Romance, it changes everything

When Bianca was 15, she attended a music camp where, given some social freedom, she was able to interact with some popular students. This led to her meeting her first boyfriend who helped her gain social status and ultimately protected her from bullies.

> *I was crying, to all the girls in my dorm—I was friends with two or three of them and then the other two were really popular girls—and I was having a sook about how no boy could ever possibly love me. And then the boys came into our dorm and . . . we were all having fun and eating snacks and stuff. And I was still really sad. But then my [now] ex-boyfriend came sat on my bed and was like, 'Why are you crying?' And I was like, 'I don't think anyone's ever gonna love me'. And then two days later, he asked me out. . . .*
>
> *I gained friends because of him. He was really popular, and I was really unpopular, and he brought me closer to his level in a way. . . .*

This safety meant it was important for her to maintain this relationship. Bianca had learnt that thinness was a prerequisite for love, so her relationship produced thin-centric thoughts.

I thought that he was more thin and more muscular than I was, and therefore . . . I needed to work harder to be thinner and more muscular than him, because—well, thinner not more muscular . . . so that we would look good together.

Navigating a romantic relationship without parental approval

Bianca's parents did not approve of her boyfriend which put a strain on her relationship with them. However, Bianca was sure that she could fix his flaws by being, "*That little ray of sunshine for him*".

They wanted us to break up pretty much the entire way through . . . he made a lot of mistakes during our relationship . . . I think my parents saw that I was trying to fix him . . . my mum would constantly be like, 'You can't fix him. But we're gonna let you try. Because you need to learn that mistake yourself'.

Sexual assault: A broader conversation (with nobody to tell it to)

Around one year into this relationship, Bianca and her boyfriend attended a party together. Her parents allowed her to go to the party, however, they were not aware that there was underage drinking.

There was a lot of . . . underage drinking. And they weren't aware of that . . . I think if they were aware of that, I wouldn't have been able to go.

At the party her boyfriend attempted to sexually assault her with the help of his friends.

I was locked in a room and his friends were holding onto the door and I couldn't get out . . . he was hanging onto my clothes and I ripped off my clothes and ran out. And then . . . he tried to physically assault me as well . . . in front of everybody—and because everyone was so intoxicated no one saw it . . . and, while it all happened, I accidentally put my hand through a piece of glass . . . that piece of glass that was broken was the only physical evidence of what happened. . . .

Bianca confronted her boyfriend; however, his response was to abuse drugs, something that she was then blamed for.

I called him the next day, crying . . . then his drug abuse got even worse . . . and it was my fault that his drug abuse got worse. Because I was the one who like, had said something to him. . . .

Bianca did not tell her parents about the assault, because she would risk exposing the information she had omitted about the party and, more importantly, she risked losing her boyfriend who dictated her social status, which already danced a very fine line between popular and pariah.

> *My parents are a huge part of my life, like we always communicate about everything, and because I couldn't communicate that to them, there has been so much shame that has gone on in the past. . . .*
>
> *I thought that they would think because I went to the party, and I was there watching him drink, that it would be my fault. . . .*
>
> *I thought that they were gonna make me break up with him. . . . I was like, 'Oh, no, don't make me break up with him. I love him'. . . . I thought that they would bring in the authorities. . . . And it was already so hard to get any freedom whatsoever. I knew that . . . if I told them, everything would be taken away.*
>
> *I already felt like I was so unlikable. I thought that if I was 'that girl whose parents wouldn't let her do anything', I would be even more unlikable.*

Bianca was restricted in who she could talk to about this. Her friends were friends she had made through her boyfriend, so telling them would risk the safety of her relationship. However, as she had broken a window at the party, Bianca realised she could tell the host of the party under the pretext of apologising. Unfortunately, this was met with nonchalance, downplaying the severity of Bianca's experience. This situation led Bianca to think that her body did not belong to her.

> *I went to the boy who had the party and I said, 'I'm sorry, I broke a piece of glass trying to get away'. . . . And I was like, 'Yeah, it was really bad, I was locked in a—in a bathroom'. And he's like, 'Oh nah, it's fine, it's fine, it's fine'. And no—it didn't happen, 'cause no one saw anything . . . after that . . . I had another little dive in body-image where I was like, 'Ah, this isn't my body anymore'.*

Self-harm: Learning to cope through the social environment

At Bianca's school, there were many people around her who were engaging in self-harm as a "coping mechanism". So, as Bianca attempted to deal with her emotional turmoil, she too used this behaviour to cope.

> *A lot of the people around me were also [self-harming] as coping mechanisms . . . there were multiple people in my group [who were] self-harming. . . .*
>
> *I was very, very secretive . . . [I did this for] maybe a year—but very irregularly throughout the year. Just whenever anything was really bad.*

Breaking up with more persons than one

When she was 17, Bianca and her boyfriend broke up. This confirmed Bianca's earlier fears, that being with him protected her from being bullied. Not only did her boyfriend's social group discard her, but the few friends that she did have before she started seeing her boyfriend, were not in her life anymore. She was once again an outsider at school.

> *I thought that being with him protected me from being bullied, which I think it did. Because then when we broke up, I got bullied again. . . .*

In grieving her relationship with her boyfriend and his school community, Bianca lost her appetite and consequently, she lost weight. Bianca's parents did not force her to eat as they usually would. They understood that sometimes it can be hard to eat when you are sad.

> *When I broke up with my high school boyfriend, I did lose a bit of weight because I just stopped eating because I was so upset. . . . I just wouldn't eat for a couple days. . . . And my parents would understand because they'd be like, 'Oh, well, you know, she's had a breakup. . . .' that's why I wasn't eating. . . .*

Completing school

Fortunately, Bianca was only weeks away from finishing her final year of school which she completed from home as recommended by her psychologist.

> *I got clearance from my psychologist at the time. She was like, 'Yeah, no, literally going to school would make everything so much worse'.*

Becoming an adult

New life contexts

Despite feeling like an imposter, Bianca did begin studying at university. Life as a university student meant she was able to manage her time more independently rather than following the rigid structure of the school week. She became involved in amateur musical theatre, working in unpaid performances. She was also employed in retail, providing her more financial independence from her parents whom she still lived with. These new contexts provided new platonic and romantic relationships, but new is not always good.

"Whirlwind" relationship

Not long after school, Bianca had a "whirlwind" relationship with a man who made her feel loved and invaluable, something she craved after high school. However, he also made her feel like a trophy, whose value is determined by her appearance.

> *It was a very short relationship, but it was a whirlwind. . . . I was 18, he was 21. And he told me that he loved me within three weeks . . . we were at a music festival, and he asked me to marry him. And I was like, 'Oh, I guess this is what love is'.*

> *He kind of kept me as his trophy in a way which definitely made me very conscious of the way I looked.*

The ephemeral relationship soon came to an end and Bianca was reminded of her high school years.

> *. . . he then hung out with the girl who used to bully me in high school, like two weeks later, and then we broke up. . . .*

Development of eating disorder behaviour

Bianca's body-image concerns were defined by a fear of being negatively perceived by a 'generalised other'.

> *I feel like the people that I have in my life are pretty strong and wouldn't leave me for something like that [putting on weight]. But I think it's purely how society sees me.*

Bianca struggled to perceive herself, something she attributed to variations in clothing sizes in ready-made clothing that categorises people as 'small', or 'extra-extra-large'. In addition to body-shaming discourse, these labels gave her new discourses to define her body.

> *When I try to perceive myself, I very much struggle . . . And I think that also ties in with the way that clothes are made . . . when you walk into a store and some places, you're small, but other places, you're an extra-large, it really makes it very confusing for how you perceive yourself.*

Musical theatre

Bianca began working in a musical theatre production just before she turned 19. This experience unfortunately reiterated the idea that being thin equates to being worthy.

> *I worked with a company who really reiterated to us, two weeks before our performance, that everyone looked disgusting on stage, and that we all should start running and doing cardio every day. . . .*
>
> *. . . They made me try on size like 16 clothing . . . I was like, 'Wait, I'm not a size 16. Why am I . . . being put in size 16 clothing?' . . . That was kind of like, making me feel like everyone perceived me as being bigger than I am . . . I didn't want to be perceived as being big.*

Friends developed eating disorders

This experience was also negative for the other cast members, some of which Bianca had become friends with. One particular friend began engaging in eating disorder behaviours following some very directed comments.

A choreographer said to her . . . 'You're not skinny enough . . . to fit into these pants'. . . . And she took that and got very, very severe anorexia. . . . I was there to help her through that . . . and I kind of picked up a lot of the traits and the negativity that she had running through her mind.

Bianca and another friend were there to support this friend; however, in time, her other friend also became obsessive in her weight-loss behaviours. The conversations between Bianca's two friends became competitive, constantly discussing what they were doing to lose weight.

One of the girls was like, 'Oh, yeah, I went to cycling. And I did it for two hours. And I burnt off like 1000 calories'. . . . Then having another friend be like, 'Oh, yeah, I'm doing my 15,000 steps a day. And I just, I just literally walk around my house. And then I go boxing'. And in my mind, I was like, '. . . I have too much going on in my life for me to be able to compete with that. . . .' And that was making me real depressed and real guilty and shameful about not being able to exercise enough . . . 'How can I counteract not exercising enough in comparison to what they're doing?' By changing my eating habits.

I wanted them to get better. . . . But hearing what they would say, I would want to be like them and do the same things that they were doing so that I could get smaller. . . .

Bianca wanted to be like her friends. She had not fit in in the past and had felt like being skinny was the key to being loved. So, she too began exercising excessively and eating less.

New relationship

During her time in the musical theatre production, Bianca also formed a relationship with her current boyfriend. He was very kind to her and did not actively encourage any weight-loss behaviours. However, Bianca's past relationships had shaped the way she behaved in her relationships.

I've always found that like, my boyfriends' weight, and like, the way they look, influences the way I feel. . . . So like, once I found out what my boyfriend weighed, and it made me feel bad . . . I was like, 'Ah, he's a man. He should be like 10 kilos heavier than me at least'. But he was only like five kilos heavier than me. And I was like, 'Oh my god, like I'm a man'.

Her boyfriend did his best to mitigate her body-image concerns and, as their relationship became more serious, her body-image concerns were no longer centred around how she looked relative to him.

Lack of control: "I felt like everything was spiralling"

Love and a sex life: As Bianca's relationship became more serious, new hurdles arose. Bianca's parents did not allow her to sleep in the same bed as her boyfriend as they actively discouraged premarital sex.

We weren't allowed to sleep in the same bed. We weren't allowed to go on holidays together.

. . . It's kind of one of those things. Like, 'If we don't talk about [sex], it doesn't exist. You won't do it'. . . . My family has always been like a wait-till-marriage kind of family. That's religion for you.

So, despite Bianca being an adult, she still had people controlling her.

COVID-19, globally out of control: While she was used to her parents controlling her, her level of control seemed far more minute when the COVID-19 pandemic began, resulting in strict rules regarding when she could leave her house, whom she could let into her house and how far away she could travel.

. . . Because of COVID and everything—like I couldn't control lockdowns, I couldn't control anything—I felt like everything was spiralling.

Unwanted attention: Bianca did not want to be negatively perceived, however, there were times when she was "positively" received in a way that made her feel equally as uncomfortable. Around the onset of her eating disorder, she was working in retail in menswear, where she received some unwanted attention.

I had a stalker at one point . . . he would come into the workplace, and literally, he would say, 'I came in just to see you'. And then he would call me beautiful, and say like, 'Oh, you're so fit, like, what do you do for exercise?' And then . . . comment on the way I looked . . . [I told my manager and] I'll specify, HE thought it was funny. I don't think a female manager would ever think that was funny.

After not receiving support from her manager, Bianca quit this job; however, this reiterated the presence of the male gaze and instilled a fear of being perceived.

Asserting control again

Bianca's life was being controlled by so many external factors, much like when she was in school and unable to control her environment, she looked to the people around her to guide her behaviour.

It's like the exact same thing [as self-harm] . . . you just want to have control over something, so like, 'I'll hurt myself instead'.

Being perceived was something so out of Bianca's control that it was exhausting for her.

I said, a lot of times . . . 'I just wish I was dead'. . . . It's more like I just want to sleep for a really, really long time. That is more preferable than being in the present moment . . . I've always wanted to be alive . . . I just wanted to not have to be perceived and go about my day like everything was okay.

Bianca already struggled with perceiving herself. So, her perceptions of herself were easily influenced by the way her friends were talking about themselves.

> *I can easily be swayed or impacted by negative body talk from other people. . . .*
>
> *I would look in the mirror back at my lowest point [and] I would see myself being like an obese balding man, which is delusional. . . . But in my mind, I was like, 'You are gross'.*
>
> *It was kinda just like that negative voice in the back of your head . . . being like . . . 'You're fat and like ugly'. . . . [the voice] was definitely me . . . it was hard to turn it off. . . . 'Cause it's kinda like, the eating disorder became me.*

She knew she could not avoid being perceived, and so eating disorder behaviours were a way for her to prove her body was hers to control. If people were going to perceive it, she was able to control how they perceived it.

> *I thought that if I lost weight, then I, then everyone would love me. And that, I would have no problems in the world and that I would actually finally be pretty.*

Bianca's eating disorder became the forefront of her life, occupying her thoughts and behaviours even while she was doing other things.

> *The only thing I could control was what I could and couldn't eat. . . .*
>
> *All I could think about was body and food . . . even when I was doing uni work, it was still in the back of my head. I was just thinking about what food I can eat that will make me lose weight.*

Eating disorders within her culture

Bianca's Italian family actively observed her body and her eating habits, praising both weight-loss and eating big meals.

> *My auntie on Mother's Day said, 'You look so good. Have you lost weight?'*

As food was a way of showing love in Bianca's family, it was difficult to avoid without offending someone.

> *I've always been a big eater . . . if I came to a family occasion and I had a much smaller plate than usual, I would get comments for sure. And like, especially when my auntie . . . she is so fixated on her body, and so fixated on everyone else's, that she's the type of person to be like, 'Oh, why aren't you eating?' And she would do it in a way that like everyone would hear. . . .*
>
> *. . . And then everyone's gonna pile on and, you know, either say positive or negative comments, or it's going to make everyone uncomfortable if I actually say what is really happening, and then I'll ruin the day. . . .*

It's one of those things where it's like, 'Okay, I'm out of control'. Again, I can't control the situation. I can't control how people perceive me or how they think about this situation.

Having an eating disorder in a way that is culturally acceptable

It was not just about people taking offence to her eating behaviours or even how they perceived her. Bianca feared that her parents would revert to methods they used in her childhood to encourage her to eat, further compromising her control.

In my family it was always, 'Oh, well, take three more bites, and then you can leave'. I felt like those childish, like habits were going to be re-implemented into my house as a grown adult.

Bianca had to reduce her food intake in a way that was socially acceptable within her household. So, when her friend had a breakup and lost weight, Bianca was reminded of when she broke up with her high school boyfriend.

She stopped eating and she lost a tonne of weight . . . I was like, 'Maybe I should go and have a breakup, so I can get really, really skinny'.

While she did not break up with her boyfriend, she realised that sadness was a reason for her to not eat within her household.

Sometimes I would hope that something sad would happen so that I wouldn't have to eat.

Bianca's eating disorder was also reinforced by people around her, encouraging her to behave in this way.

I didn't eat a substantial meal for like three days. And someone said to me like, 'Oh you look so good and so thin, like I can see your bones'. And I was like, 'Oh, you can see my bones? Like that's so good'. . . . Thinking back on that . . . why would you want to see your bones? Like . . . when I see like someone who has . . . absolutely no muscle or fat on their body . . . I don't want to look like that. . . . I don't ever want to be that thin, but I feel like I do want to be that, you know, 'Instagram thin', or like, that 'actress thin'.

Recovery

Me and my friends who have eating disorders . . . we always thought, 'Oh, it's not bad enough to go get help'.

More important things to do: New life contexts

When Bianca began studying at a post-graduate level at university, she realised that she could not perform at the standard she needed to without getting better.

I couldn't afford to go and be at the gym for three hours a day . . . I had to go back to eating because I had things to do.

Family facilitating recovery

Bianca eventually asked her mother for help.

I called my mum into my room . . . and I just broke down and I was like, 'I don't want to eat anything. I just want to be skinny'. And she was like, 'Okay, like we're booking in right now to go see someone'. . . . She was like, 'Okay . . . we're sending you to therapy. . . . We'll pay for it. . . .' I wouldn't have done that if I didn't reach out to her . . . I think that's the most important thing, having a good support system. It's very helpful.

I've actively taken on therapy and like, I don't passively sit in therapy and expect the therapist to fix me . . . I think the driving force for me was like, 'I just want to be able to eat with my friends and family and not feel like shit'.

Bianca learned to question her fear of being negatively perceived, as well as methods to change the eating disorder voice that occupied her thoughts.

My therapist has been like, 'Okay, so what if someone on the street sees you? What are you going to feel?' And I'm like, 'Well, it depends on how they perceive me'. And she's like, 'Well, why do you care? What's that gonna do for you?' And I'm like, 'Literally, it's gonna do nothing for me'. But I'm still like, 'Uh, they need to love me, everyone must love me'.

Something that I've found really useful is assigning a character to . . . the negative voice in your head that is like, your 'eating disorder voice' . . . my least favourite actor is Willem Dafoe . . . so whenever I hear, like the eating disorder voice, I picture it as Willem Dafoe . . . and I tell him to 'fuck off' . . .

. . . it's still my mind saying, 'Oh, don't eat'. But if I just stick a cardboard cutout face [of Willam Dafoe] on that voice in my mind—I'm like, 'Shut up'.

I think it's because you blame yourself for having this disorder. So, if you have something else to blame it on, then it's not a 'you' problem.

Opening up to parents

Bianca had gone years without telling her parents about her ex-boyfriend sexually assaulting her, which had put a strain on their relationship. So, when she did finally tell them, her relationship with them was able to be repaired.

I ended up telling them about what happened. . . . And that opened up a door for me to actually start living my life again, because I was like, 'Okay I finally don't have anything to hide'.

Bianca was able to have honest conversations with her parents about her body-image concerns, her relationship with her boyfriend, and sex. This shifted the way they treated her. They allowed her more freedom in her actions which, in turn, helped her to trust them more. This helped Bianca's recovery as she was able to control her life more broadly, rather than just being able to control what she ate.

> *Having a now sex positive household . . . it's just a way better environment where I feel like I can actually voice how I feel about things and voice like negative thoughts and not feel as judged for it.*
> *. . . Now I can jet off to a different state and live at [my boyfriend's] house for two weeks . . . they definitely trust me a lot more and therefore less controlling.*

Spending less time with friends with eating disorders

Bianca actively distanced herself from her friends with eating disorders to allow herself space to recover.

> *There was a period of time where we pretty much didn't speak, because we were all like, 'Okay, we all need to get better. And we can't get better if we're making each other's behaviours worse'.*

Feminist perspective

Bianca adapted a feminist perspective when navigating her life, considering how she is perceived by women rather than by men.

> *Society pushes that women need to adhere to like the male fantasy. And I think this year I've realised that the male fantasy and the male gaze is just utter shit, and I started living for women. I went through a phase where I deleted every single person who made me feel bad about myself off of Instagram. . . . I didn't see people coming up on my feed that weren't real.*
> *It's not a 'me' issue. It's a societal issue. Like, I'm now looking at my body with more of a neutrality than like positivity. . . .*
> *It's just like the switch of mindset to not be like, 'Yeah, I'm curvy. And I've got beautiful big boobs'. . . . It's more like, 'Oh my body helps me to move, my body helps keep me healthy'.*

Navigating life after recovery

"I would rather just be . . . a floating head—if I could be"

Bianca remains adamant that she would rather not be perceived visually; however, she is now navigating her life with the desire to be perceived based on her clothing choices rather than her body.

> *I would prefer not to be perceived as like a physical entity. I would rather just be like, just like a floating head—if I could be . . . I would prefer that people commented on things like, 'Oh, you're so funny' or, you know, 'You're so smart', than like, 'Oh, you look good'.*

> *Like with my clothing choices, I feel like I try to stand out a little bit more. But inherently . . . I want to be perceived in a way that's positive.*

Re-establishing relationships and behaviours that defined her eating disorder

Bianca has been able to reintroduce the relationships and behaviours that fuelled her eating disorder, without them interfering with her ability to proceed with the rest of her day. She can now see her friends who had eating disorders without her weight-loss behaviours emerging.

> *It's like before we all had eating disorders . . . we just hang out and we just talk about everything in life that isn't related to the eating disorder.*

She can now do behaviours that used to be paramount in the maintenance of her eating disorder, such as looking in the mirror and going to the gym, without them becoming 'disordered'.

> *I literally looked at myself naked today . . . and I thought, 'Not bad'. . . . I look the exact same, it's just, I'm looking at my body in a different way now.*
>
> *Instead of going to the gym with the active, like, manifestation that, 'I need to get skinnier'. I started going to the gym with the active manifestation of, 'I'm doing this for me because it releases those happy hormones, and it makes me feel good on the inside, not look good on the outside'.*

Thoughts to engage in eating disorder behaviours are now fleeting, not 'cured'

Bianca used her eating disorder behaviours as a way for her to deal with stress for a substantial amount of time, so, when she becomes stressed, she still feels inclined to use these behaviours again.

> *My boyfriend is in a different state, and I can't go see him because of COVID. I feel a complete loss of control. . . .*
>
> *. . . Because my friend passed away . . . I don't want to eat and it doesn't come from a place of like, 'I want to be skinny'. It comes from a place of like, 'I physically can't bring myself to eat'.*
>
> *I think maybe it's more comfortable to go back to something you already know. . . . I'll always know what it feels like to be insecure about my body . . . but this is the first time I've had to grieve the loss of a friend.*
>
> *Like you're going to lose weight from being sad. And I shouldn't look at that as a positive. But . . . I did have that thought.*

Despite these thoughts occurring regularly, Bianca is able to allow these thoughts to pass by without becoming obsessive or succumbing to the desires.

She actively reminds herself of the responsibilities in her life that require her to be well.

> *Knowing that I have to keep going, like, I don't have a choice . . . that's how I'm getting through it.*

What we can learn from Bianca

Bianca's eating disorder propagated from the patriarchal society in which she lives. It was led by fear of negative perceptions and desire to be thin and accepted. She felt a need to be perceived positively in both her body and her temperament, which highlights the presence of a generalised other in contemporary western society.

Her restrictions surrounding discourse with her parents, particularly following her experience of sexual assault made moving past this experience difficult as without voicing these thoughts to an audience, there are no consequences and they persist.

Once Bianca was able to discuss her past traumatic experiences with her parents, her environment became less restrictive and she was able to recover. She also used feminist perspectives to reframe the cultural context she was living in, meaning her insecurities became a 'society' issue and not a 'Bianca' issue.

9 Erica's story
Mother knows best

Restrictive eating and excessive exercise were modelled to Erica from a young age, particularly by her mother, who was obsessed with being thin and equated appearance with success. When Erica went to therapy as an early adult for unrelated reasons, she was diagnosed with anorexia nervosa, but struggled to disentangle the thoughts she had about herself as a person, from the thoughts about her body. The disordered behaviour could be masqueraded whilst attending acting school, almost like a Band-Aid waiting to be ripped off. A tumultuous relationship breakdown and loss of identity was the catalyst for Erica's recovery.

I feel like for me, in my house growing up, appearance and how you look is a real measure of success.

Childhood

Erica learnt most of her restrictive eating and body-image practices by observing those around her in her early, formative years.

My mum, for example. It's just her as a person. She was always really, really big into that type of stuff. Always going to the gym, that really caring a lot about her health. . . . A lot of my childhood she'd go to the gym almost every day. So before I was at school, if she was going to the gym, she would take us to the creche. The girls who worked there would come and nanny me as well at nights, because we were there all the time.

Mum, she used to pride herself on that behaviour as well. I remember when my younger sister was in a pram, so she wouldn't have even been 1, my mum ran the City to Bay with her in the pram. . . . But she had three kids, so there's a point in your life where your body doesn't bounce back to what you were at pre-30. So I think she definitely didn't like the fact that she had gained a bit of weight.

I've always kind of grown up around a diet culture. It was constantly between, maybe we're doing fad dieting or working really hard at the gym. Always complaining about her weight or complaining about her appearance, blah blah blah.

DOI: 10.4324/9781003453918-11

Erica spoke about how her mother would criticise her, which became the template in which she began to view herself.

> *If I was ever wearing anything that slightly showed my shape she would always comment, without a doubt, she would always comment. . . . So it was always about appearances rather than asking, 'how you going?' kind of thing. And she would always comment if she noticed that I was losing weight or anything. She'd always comment but she'd always say, 'you're looking really skinny' rather than 'oh, is everything okay?'*

Even when the comments were not directed at her weight, another element of appearance was emphasised over internal qualities.

> *I remember when I 'properly' started restricting intentionally, and I got really bad skin as well. I guess that was a by-product of the way I was eating. But I remember that really vividly as well because my mum was obsessed with my skin. Just saying things like 'your skin is terrible' and stuff. So then again that played into the narrative of your appearance being the most important thing.*

Erica's sister is two years younger than her, and her mother often compared the sisters against one another.

> *My sister naturally has a fast metabolism. She's also got quite a naturally flat stomach and big bum kind of area. And it's the thing that is so on trend. It's the desirable body. And having my mum always comparing us like, 'your sister has the good stomach, you have the good legs' kind of thing. Stuff like those kind of comments, and come summer always making comments about how tiny my sister's waist is or how tiny she is. Again, I don't think she does it on purpose, but it is still around your appearance being before anything else.*

Reflecting now on these comments, Erica can identify how they continue to impact the sister's self-image today.

> *My sister hates her legs. And I hate my stomach. But neither of us even really look at other parts of our body. . . . If we both go to the gym, my sister mainly works her legs, has such a focus on that body part of her legs but for me, it's the complete opposite. I'm always doing cardio and ab workouts, targeting my stomach.*

Although Erica doesn't believe her sister struggled with the same eating disorder she did, she can recall times where she made similar critical comments to their mother.

> *This was quite a big one. I was really young, I reckon I was 4 or something. I remember my sister called me fat. And I remember sobbing, I was so distraught at that. And I remember distinctly having memories of looking in the mirror and sucking in my stomach at a really young age. Really, really young. And I remember*

my mum asked what I was doing when I was getting ready for something, asking why I was sucking in and I said because [my sister] thinks I'm fat. I remember that vividly. Which is weird because I was so young.

From Erica's mother's perspective, beauty was the definition of success, resulting in access to increased resources and relationships. This constant pressure to maintain a certain image offered Erica little opportunity for escape.

I'm the tallest out of my mum and my sister, so naturally I am gonna weigh a bit more. I remember how my mum would complain about her weight saying, 'Oh, I'm like this many kilos' or something. And I remember thinking I weigh more than that . . . my mum saying that it's a bad thing for her to be that way. That means that I'm overweight. If she thinks she's fat, then she must think I'm fat.

I think I have always had this thing of subconsciously not wanting to be this or that. And having that ingrained in me from such a young age.

You know, if you can look good that means you're doing really well and you're gonna get liked by people.

Besides her mother and sister, Erica recollects her primary school experiences that contributed to her poor self-esteem.

I was bullied in primary school by my friends. I always think friend bullying is always worse than just a typical bully . . . having friends exclude you and bitch about you, and that kind of uncertainty is almost worse. I think this comes back to the inconsistency. Because, well, they're my friends sometimes. But they also say really awful things about me. Whereas the typical bully is just always mean, you know what you're getting, you know what to expect more. It was unpredictable. It was always, 'Oh, are they going to like me today?'

I would call up my friend and ask, 'Are you mad at me?' and she'd say 'Yeah, I am' and I'd ask, 'Why are you mad at me?' She'd reply, 'I don't know' and that was literally the conversation. I'd say, 'Oh, okay, are you gonna talk to me at school tomorrow?' And she'd say, 'I don't know', I'd just be like 'Oh, okay' and then having raging anxiety.

During this time in her life, Erica hadn't developed the skills to rationalise why the people she cared about were treating her this way. This behaviour was normalised and modelled by her mother.

Girls got bitchy at around 9 to 10. And I was constantly anxious. And I look now, and I can identify that and understand, no wonder I was feeling like shit all the time. And that's why I probably didn't like myself very much.

I didn't have the capacity to be like, 'Oh, these people are just awful people. They're not your friends. They're not nice people'. I thought, 'Oh, these are the most amazing people in the whole world. And they're my friends and I love them so much. And I hold them to that high regard. If they don't like me, I must be a terrible person because XYZ'.

Erica did not feel she could respond in the negative ways her peers were due to her value of being a good girl.

> *I was known as a good child. I remember when I was a kid and we went strawberry picking. The staff told us that you can't eat any strawberries when you're out there. And my parents would just eat the strawberries and say it was fine, but I refused to eat any strawberries out there because they told us that we can't do it. And so I'm just gonna wait until we pay for these strawberries and then I will eat it.*
>
> *I was really scared about how people perceived me. I was always really anxious about not doing the right thing, and even other people not doing the right thing. Or people not liking me or getting in trouble and stuff like that. That was a massive fear of mine. I would hate having any attention on me at all. I could not stand being embarrassed and feeling like people were looking at me.*

Erica attributes her lack of understanding of some social normalities to being the eldest child. Therefore, she was extremely concerned about how other people perceived her, even as a young child.

> *I think it definitely has a lot to do with growing up as a kid. I guess being the oldest child, having to go to school first, and not having anyone above me to pave the way, and really having to navigate that by myself. I remember being in primary school, and really feeling like I didn't know anyone and really feeling that I'm not friends with anyone. . . . I remember as a really little kid, around 5. I think I was being rude to my mum a lot of the time. I remember my mum told my teacher and then my teacher sat me down and spoke to me, asking why are you mean to your mum? And I remember being mortified and being so angry at my mum. And I was like, 'Why did you tell her that I was being rude? Now she thinks I'm a terrible person'. Being so upset about how my teacher thought of me.*
>
> *I don't really know where that came from. I probably assume maybe my mum because she also has a completely different personality out of the house to in the house. I feel like people who meet my mum probably think she's the nicest person, never cranky. I feel like she comes across as really open, really friendly, which is to other people. But then inside the house, she's got a lot of anger in her, she's a very angry person. She's nowhere near as laid back. So I don't know if maybe subconsciously, that might be something that I picked up on. There's a different personality for how you want people to perceive you or something. But I really don't know, I feel like I've always just had to present myself in an inconsistent way to please others.*

Secondary school

In secondary school, Erica started to develop a sense of how she could get people to accept her and like her. At first, it took the form of mimicking her mother's behaviour.

> *I was obsessed with being healthy. I remember when I was 14 I said I will never drink alcohol ever. I vowed that I was just gonna eat clean and treat my body like a*

temple. And I wouldn't have been liked. But I think it was quite to the point where, you know, if we had cake for anything, I would not eat cake. I was like, 'No, no, no, I don't eat bad foods'. On my 15th birthday I said, 'I don't want a cake, I want a watermelon cake'. So I got a watermelon and put yoghurt and fruit on top and said this is my cake. And I said and probably believed, I love this cake.

But in terms of my mental health at this time, it was actually pretty good. I was doing really good in my sports and winning medals and everything. I was at a stage where I had a lot of friends and I thought that this would be my whole life. But then that kind of diffused because there was a time where friends were changing, I think after I turned 15. Then it was the same year that my year level at school started to drink at parties.

When things felt out of control in her life, the most natural thing for her to do was focus on the elements of life that were within her control.

When I was 16, I remember I was doing sports, I was doing acting and it's all that thing of relevance in my life at that point. They were the biggest things for me, but I got really overloaded, really anxious all the time. I was talking to a boy, but it wasn't solid, it was not a solid relationship or an official one. That might have caused me the most anxiety because I was so unsure. And I think it just caused me to fixate on things that I knew I could definitely control.

Erica had to quickly switch from being incredibly health conscious to trying to keep up with what was considered cool by her peers.

But I think this change definitely played an element into being anxious a lot of the time, and as well as that, I wasn't eating lunch. So I would get drunk really quickly and blackout. So I wouldn't remember half of my weekend. So I think that definitely had an element of stressing me out. So I would worry about, 'What did I do? What did I do while I was blacked out?' Then it was all about regaining control back from Monday to Friday, feeling like I needed to do everything, getting good grades, still wanting to maintain that as well. I remember I was doing my sport in the early mornings, then I had acting after school, I'd be at high school doing extracurriculars from 5am to 5:30pm, which is massive for a 16-year-old to be doing that much work and stuff, and then to be going out on the weekends. And then literally killing brain cells by blacking out and not remembering things and trying to maintain that kind of life.

And it was fun, but it was also stressful. I don't know, it was definitely doing what everyone else was doing. There was definitely an element of stress. I think not knowing what I had done or if I had pissed someone off, that was stressful.

I would keep going because I think there was a fear of missing out but also a fear of not knowing what happened on the weekend and getting to school on Monday and not having been there and people having that memory without me and being excluded from whatever. I think at the time it was, 'Yes, I do genuinely want to be doing this', but I think it was driven more by a fear of missing out than wanting to be there.

The fear of missing out meant that for Erica to avoid disappointing anyone, she had to adapt her behaviour accordingly.

My parents didn't know how much I was partying. I was trying hard to maintain these different images. I would tell them maybe every fourth weekend that I was going to a party but really it was every weekend, but I would tell them I was going to a sleepover or going to someone's house to study or something. Trying to maintain that life while being one person from Monday to Friday then another on the weekends.

Looking back many years later at the many commitments she made for herself, Erica thinks she may have over-committed to avoid the criticism she was being exposed to at home and seek other sources of validation.

I don't think it was ever a conscious choice to be like, I'm getting out of the house. But I think it just kind of happened. I got into the school through sports. And then I joined theatre. And then it was, 'Oh, I'm just doing these things'. But also I've made these two massive commitments that I don't want to drop either. And I think what I do is I overload my schedule to avoid thinking and feeling about things. Which is a similar reason why I have an eating disorder, to not then deal with the feelings that I am actually feeling.

Validation is one of the most important things to Erica, and she attributes this to the experiences of desperately seeking validation while being repeatedly rejected. Her sense of self relied entirely on how she could be of use to other people and what other people thought of her.

It's a very intangible thing, I think. To say validation, but it's not as superficial as, 'Oh, yeah, I get validated'. I think some validation of, 'Oh, I'm doing a good thing for someone', but I think it just gives me purpose. I think the idea of being a good friend and serving people, for lack of a better word, always being ready to help. I don't even think it's about the return. I think the return is them liking you.

It's almost validating that I'm doing a good job of being a human. Maybe this sounds kind of odd, or it sounds superficial, but I think for me, a massive part of my values is my friendships and the relationships I hold. It is really important to me to be a good friend. And I think as well as that for me, I don't like the idea of people feeling like shit, because I think I feel like shit a lot of the time. And I really don't like the idea of people feeling unsupported. Because I think because I feel like that, I don't want other people to feel like that. So I think for me, I guess I put a lot of my heart and soul into the friendships that I have, and the time and energy I give people, I really like to think that I do put a lot of effort into that.

But I don't really leave myself much when I give a friendship to someone. So I think for me, if someone would not like me, it would be such a personal attack to my psyche. And so I think I would definitely question my worth as a person. Rather than maybe normal people just thinking, 'Oh, they don't like me, I'm not for everyone'. I think for me, if I give you something and you're gonna piss off with it, it

really shakes my core because I think, 'Oh, I've done something really, really wrong.
What have I done wrong?' And it makes me question my self-worth.

Constantly adapting her behaviour meant that Erica had to become a master of
control to meet the expectations she had set for herself.

> *When I do feel like my life is out of control, I go to what I know is successful, and*
> *that's my appearance and that's what my worth is.*
>
> *I don't like myself. So I think because of that, I need people to like me to be liked*
> *and to feel liked. Because in order to be loved and liked, I feel like I need other people*
> *to do that. Because I feel like I can't give that to myself.*
>
> *And I think that's why an eating disorder thrives in me, because it gives me that*
> *sense of accomplishing that for myself. Being like, 'Look what you've done, you've*
> *made yourself like yourself, you've done that all by yourself'. I think for me, I actu-*
> *ally don't really like myself very much at all or my own company. So I think if other*
> *people like me, and I am with other people, and overworking, constantly being busy,*
> *I'm not stuck with myself.*

Graduation and acting school

After high school, Erica studied at acting school and eating habits stabilised. In
acting school, there was less pressure and competition from her peers around
looks.

> *I just genuinely needed food because my value of being a better actor was greater than*
> *my value of looking a certain way.*
>
> *So I was in acting school, and I was getting a lot of validation from being there and*
> *doing really well. The other girls were quite a bit bigger than me. So I think in terms*
> *of comparison every day . . . I know that sounds really bad. But to me, I was like,*
> *'Well, the only thing that we can compete against is our acting'. And because I was*
> *in a relationship, it wasn't like I was trying to get someone or beat out this girl who*
> *looks better than me. There wasn't that element of needing to be better than anybody.*

Day-to-day at acting school Erica was focused on acting performance. When
shows were coming up and she had to perform in front of an audience, she lost
her appetite and reduced her eating. This was similar to in high school, but the
difference was she had friends in acting school, and when the performance was
over she would eat again.

> *Every time I had a show or something, those behaviours would definitely come*
> *up. When I get anxious, naturally, I lose my appetite. So whenever I had a show,*
> *I would lose my appetite because of the show . . . the less I ate, the more anxious I'd*
> *get, the more anxious I'd get the less I'd eat. The anorexia would come in and say,*
> *'Let's control this to make you less anxious' even though the lack of eating makes*
> *you more anxious.*

But those anxious periods were very situational. As soon as the show ended. It was like, 'Oh, okay, I'm not anxious anymore, It's the end of term, I'm with my friends, I'm having a good time'. . . . I think having someone there on the sidelines, such a strong support network on the sidelines, I'd have someone who was a little bit more there to just kind of go, 'Let's bring it back down'. . . . Doing shows was so validating, after shows I would be very not anxious and very calm. And all that anxiety kind of left. I was getting a lot more validation in other ways and areas.

Finishing acting school brought uncertainty, because there was a lack of employment opportunities in the local acting industry, and she no longer had the structure of class and seeing friends every day. She found that returning to her other methods of control was the most natural thing to do, to keep busy, which was easy after being accepted into university.

While I was at drama school, everything was very stable while I was there. I think graduating, you then graduate into complete instability. You don't have a job. You don't graduate and know you've got a job afterwards. You might get a job, but it might only be four weeks of work. And then you might not ever work in that field again. So I think for me I was really stressed.

I remember waking up after my final performance and thinking 'God, was that my final day of acting school?' I did my final performance, then went out for drinks after with everyone. Next I remember waking up really early. I think I got four hours of sleep. I was really hungry too. I woke up and I remember thinking 'Oh my god, I'm gonna be really depressed. This is going to really send me'. Then I just thought 'Nope, that's not what's going to happen'. And I wrote this massive to-do list. And I shot up and started having a shower. I told my boyfriend I was gonna smash a bunch of work and he was like, 'Uh, are you okay?' That same morning was when I found out I got into Uni, which is such a weird coincidence. So that was the morning, when I got into Uni. And I thought, 'Oh, wow'. I was happy. Going straight from acting school into a degree. So I was like yeah, 'I got this'.

She was comfortable in her relationship and felt this contributed to her eating disorder lying dormant.

I remember I said it to my boyfriend, and I was like, 'Sometimes I can be a bit angry'. And this is when we were dating for a little while. Obviously, in my mind, we were gonna get married, he was gonna be there forever. I was saying, 'Sometimes I can just be a little bit angry and be a bit moody'. But I said, 'It's not because of you'. I'm only that kind of person around my parents, my sister, my immediate family and him, because I would see them all the time. And it felt like around these people, I can maybe not be that. So it was the constant identity that I had with my sister, with my mum, with my dad, with my brother. And that sounds a bit weird, but it didn't matter as much what they thought about me as other people, because I knew they were always there.

However, this meant the dormancy was susceptible to being interrupted. Erica uncharacteristically cheated on her partner while she was out, following which they had an on-and-off relationship. Erica lost her appetite, and she had thoughts about returning to her eating disorder.

> *Being in acting school and having a boyfriend and doing all these things put a Band-Aid on [the eating disorder] for three years. And then as soon as that all kind of crumbled the Band-Aids ripped off and ripped the scab with it.*
>
> *There was still quite a lot of uncertainty in my life and a lot of just feeling really not okay. Then I got really, really drunk one night and kissed a boy who wasn't my boyfriend. I remember though I straight away went and told him. I told him everything and we were like, 'What should we do? Should we go on a break?'. We weren't really sure.*
>
> *I physically couldn't eat. It wasn't a choice not to eat. When my dad bought me an Up&Go, he asked me 'Can you please eat this?' Because I was just so unwell mentally and just so tired. And he was like, 'Can you just please, just try to eat this? It's got protein. It's an Up&Go, please'. It took me two hours to try and finish it just from sheer anxiety.*
>
> *I remember not being able to eat and it was from anxiety. Not being able to physically eat from being so anxious and nervous. It was almost this little cauldron, and it was bubbling and all came back. Like 'Remember me? Remember how much control we had? Remember when we weren't eating? And how under control things were?' My mind was just like, 'Oh hey, it's been a while, I remember you, you helped me so much. I like you. You helped me not feel anxious. You helped give me purpose'.*

Erica's identity was so strongly associated with and reliant on who she was to other people—her boyfriend, her friends, her study peers. But now she was no longer studying acting and her new career path was uncertain. Erica and her boyfriend broke up because she had done this 'bad' thing, and she lost many friends in the process. The eating disorder returned.

> *Then we eventually broke up, it was very tumultuous, very on and off. It was very toxic and very push and pull. I felt like a terrible person. I remember thinking, this is so out of character. I couldn't figure out why I did it. Why did that happen? And then I went to therapy because I was so incredibly anxious and stressed and I thought something about this restricting doesn't seem right to me anymore. I don't want to deal with this again. Because I knew what it was like, I knew how bad it had gotten when I was younger. It came as quite a shock to me how easy it was to slip back into that habit.*
>
> *I guess my thought process was 'instead of maybe the people in your life are not liking you because of you, they don't like you because you're fat'. And it was like, 'Ah, that makes sense. This is so tangible. Now if you lose weight, everyone will like you again. I'll be happy, I'll be this, I'll be that, I'll be everything I want to be. People will want me, and my boyfriend will want me back, my friends will want me. No one can say anything bad about me because I will be perfect'.*

Why my eating disorder flared up so much when I broke up with my boyfriend. And when I dropped acting school, because I lost so much of my identity, because I wasn't a girlfriend, and I wasn't an acting student. And those were the two things that I held in such high regard of who I was as a person. 'Who am I? Well, I'm a girlfriend. I'm a friend. I'm an academic student'.

So when I lost my boyfriend and lost heaps of friends in the process, and I was really unsure of the career path I was taking, it was like everything that I put my value on it kind of got crushed beneath. And then I was just like, 'Oh, I'm just kind of stuck with myself'. So it was so easy to just jump back into all those habits that maybe were still kind of dormant.

Therapy and recovery

Erica went to therapy to talk about her relationship problems and why she cheated on her boyfriend. The therapist referred her to another therapist—a specialist in body-image.

I broke up with my boyfriend, but it genuinely took going to a therapist to understand I made one mistake. That I'm not a terrible person. For me to not think I was the spawn of Satan. Because I genuinely thought I was an evil human being, I can't believe I've done this. And it took a lot for me to realise that, that I had made one mistake. But it was almost like that one mistake I had made me feel as though my whole life was not worth it.

I went to therapy, and I was in my first consultation appointment, and my eating wasn't the reason I was there, I was subconsciously thinking of that I guess but it wasn't the main issue I wanted to talk about. I was talking about my relationship and where I'd gone wrong and how I didn't know why I did what I did. And the therapist was trying to explore that with me, and she said something along the lines of, 'I think deep down you know why you did it'. And she said that unless I was absolutely paralytic drunk, which I wasn't, I would have done it for a reason whether I knew it or not. Then it slowly boiled down to the moment, when we were chatting, and I realised that it was—a feeling of not being wanted.

We had been together for around two and a half years, and there was that element of comfortableness. I remember that night I felt really wanted by the guy I kissed. I remember being out and I felt really confident, I looked really nice and so many people complimented me. I posted a photo of myself to my Instagram story and so many people replied to it saying that I looked amazing. I remember distinctly looking to see if my boyfriend had seen it, and he had but he didn't message me. No big deal but I remember seeing it and being like, 'Okay there are guys that I don't even know messaging me, saying I look amazing'. Never a good enough reason to kiss someone else, but it was my mind at the time. When I was out that night I had never had so much attention. It sounds so dramatic. I was at this table with a bunch of guys, I think five of them. And I remember looking around and thinking, 'I literally could have had any of these guys that I wanted'.

I got progressively drunker, and I was talking to this guy who he and his girlfriend had just broken up. And I asked why they broke up and he said that he didn't get on with her family, they didn't like him and they were expecting them not to work out. He went on to say how her family was religious and he wasn't, and they didn't like him because of that as well. And he said, 'How can I have a relationship with someone when their family doesn't like me? How can I expect it to work out in the end?' and I remember sitting there relating to what he said so much. He was in the exact situation I was in with my boyfriend and his family.

So I remember explaining this whole situation to my therapist and she said that she thinks that there is something much deeper going on, something related to my worth and my appearance. She told me about this woman who works really well with body-image issues and things like that, and she thinks I should go and talk to her. . . . For me, I think I thought, 'I'll just go to therapy, and just get some tips when it comes to how to reduce anxiety, and I'll be fine'. And then going in, kind of unpacking it all made me realise that it was so much more embedded in me.

Erica's body-image therapist helped her to see the harm in her eating habits and helped her on the road to recovery. Her therapist taught her how to 'externalise' her eating disorder thoughts.

Part of my recovery is identifying 'that voice' as an outside thing, identifying that as 'anorexia' rather than just thinking that it's myself. It very much feels like obeying the rules of something else, rather than my own thoughts and feelings. . . . It definitely infiltrates my own inner monologue.

I always want to be healthy, go to the gym, eat well. But when I'm feeling okay those behaviours just aren't as prominent. And the voice just wasn't as loud. . . . It's not like, 'Oh, now it's here. Now, it's not here'. It's probably somewhat constant. It's just more about draining it out, or putting it to the side and actively ignoring it and thinking I'm just not gonna listen to you right now.

Erica recognised that food played a role in social relationships and in order to maintain friendships with people, it would involve food to some degree. In her recovery, she focused on how she valued her social relationships which alleviated some stress associated with eating.

I think for me as well, maintaining good relationships and friendships with people is a massive part of my values. So, I feel like food is a massive part of social things. So, for me it was important that it made it easier to eat.

Erica was hesitant to tell her family about her eating disorder, especially given the role her mother had in its development.

I don't want them to know because I don't want them to monitor what I'm eating. . . . It's definitely a sense of wanting people to not look at me differently.

In the end, Erica's symptoms were reduced enough to not meet criteria for a diagnosis any more. However, she discussed how therapy did not help her address some of the problems that she continues to face that led to using the behaviour in the first place. She is concerned that stress being unexpectedly exacerbated in the future may lead her to using these behaviours again, and that she can't consider herself truly recovered.

10 Sally's story

Serious journos talk about lip filler

Sally identified with having various eating disorders over time, and she wondered if her recovery was just a different kind of eating disorder. She was always complimented for being tall and thin "like a model" and became anxious about losing this value from age 13. She learnt many behaviours from her father, who was obsessed with exercise, dieting and healthy eating. Her eating and exercising first became problematic in her final year of school, when she had nothing else to do in response to stress at home and school. Her disorder improved in her 20s after entering a long-term relationship with a partner who taught her to enjoy food. Sally attended therapy but she never spoke about her disorder, so she was never formally diagnosed and treated. Perhaps this is why she relied less on abstract mental health discourses to make sense of her experience, and more easily linked social and societal contexts to her behaviour.

Childhood

"I valued myself on being tall and thin, because that's all that I thought I had"

Sally's father was "obsessed" with dieting, exercise and thinness. Sally did not gain weight across childhood, so she ate freely, except for joining her sister and father in vegetarianism at age 13 for ethical reasons. Sally worried that her height was too masculine, but her parents assured her that she looked like a model.

> *My relationship with food . . . it always used to be really good when I was younger . . . I had a really fast metabolism so I never thought about food . . . I didn't care what I ate but I always valued being skinny. . . . [Dad] he's fat phobic. He always talks about people's weight . . . always thinking about ways to lose weight. He was on juice cleanses . . . drinks special healthy smoothies . . . he made me and my sister exercise with him . . . mum always feeling inadequate and feeling like she needed to lose weight . . . he was sexist to my mum, when she cut her hair, he called her a man.*
>
> *I always thought that I was really ugly . . . always a head taller than the boys that I went to school with and I had a cropped haircut so I felt quite masculine. . . .*

DOI: 10.4324/9781003453918-12

I think my parents were like, 'It's okay, don't worry about it, they're all losers, you're going to be tall and beautiful, and you're going to look like a model, so it's okay' . . . never made comments about my body that was bad, but the good comments . . . leave an impression that if you're not that, what are you?

"Endure it, lock the door, leave, no, there was no stopping it, he's not never gonna stop"

Sally's earliest memories are of her father's alcoholism. Her father drank in excess every weekend until he would cry, argue, verbally abuse the family, hurt himself, drive drunk, neglect his children and put them at risk.

He would just get so drunk that he couldn't be a parent. We would have to take care of him . . . if we said anything to oppose him, it would be bad . . . outside of all of the drunken behaviour, he wasn't a good dad, he was really manipulative and he always used to guilt trip me and my sister . . . but we thought that was normal. So I don't think we avoided it. I thought that's how people interacted with their children . . . we thought that every family fought all the time . . . maybe that's why I was so unstable because it didn't feel like a stable place to grow up in that house.

"She copped it more when he was drunk . . . she was always the first point of call because she was older"

Sally's sister was one year her senior and had issues with eating and her body since age 10. Their mother arranged for her to see a psychologist from a young age because she cut herself and acted aggressively towards others. Sally looked up to her sister. They were similar in many ways, but they also competed. Her sister looked out for her, but she could be violent towards Sally too.

She dealt with what I dealt with at home, but I was hidden from a lot . . . she saw it throughout our whole childhood . . . because they knew that she knew, they didn't hide it as much from her. . . . I was more preoccupied with myself . . . but she was very attentive . . . because she was the oldest sister I think she felt like she had to take care of me . . . taking me out and away.

"No family, it was just us . . . the people that lived there had so much money that problems didn't exist and there was no community"

Sally's immediate family relocated to an international Asian city when she was 5 years old, so they had no relationships outside of their school and work contexts. Their network consisted largely of migrants or wealthy people travelling on temporary working visas.

These traumatic things happened, we had no one to lean on . . . only one family knew about it, and we leaned on them . . . we had been friends for so long and her parents knew my parents, they knew my dad, and her mum was an alcoholic. So I think that's kind of why we got along because we understood each other. And my mum trusted that family and so my mum would leave us with them, or we would go to them, because it would be easier not to have to explain everything, because they would know.

I went to a really wealthy international school and no one had any problems because everyone had a lot of money . . . these kids are so rich, their parents are always away or their parents are busy, so I knew kids whose parents didn't even live in [the city] and they lived with butlers . . . there was so much money people didn't know how to talk to people about problems . . . it was all a façade, and no one really wanted to talk, and there were no real problems, and it just wasn't real.

"If they divorced, he would fight for custody, and we would be split over two countries"

Sally observed no love or affection between her parents. Her mother had little influence over her father's behaviour, and Sally's mother endured the marriage to avoid a custody battle.

She didn't want to be with him. She said that there were problems from the very beginning of their relationship . . . she was seriously considering divorce. I reckon I was maybe 10 and we were already there, and she was like, 'It is not possible, their lives will be torn apart' . . . she thought the easiest thing to keep us safe was just to put up with him.

Never saw them in love and it was a bad relationship. While I love my mum and I think it's super brave that she put up with him for 18 years, I'm also curious as to how that has impacted me and my sister, like watching that relationship actually fall apart and them not doing anything.

"We'll stay for as long as we can, we'll give them the best education and opportunities"

Her parents initially relocated for her father's work, but they stayed for the education opportunities granted by her mother's employment as a teacher. Her mother taught at an affluent international school, and her daughters were able to attend fee-free. Sally had little privacy from her mother, and her mother put pressure on her to achieve academically.

There's no way that any teacher would be able to afford those school fees . . . mum and dad made the decision like 'they'll get a great education if [mum] continues to teach here, why don't we just stay'. . . . Mum always put a lot of pressure on me academically. . . . I'm happy that she expects a lot of me, but she expects a lot of me! And I think that's where a lot of my anxiety comes from. Because she taught at my high school, she knew what I was doing all the time, she knew what grades I was getting. . . . She knew everything. . . . She was like, 'I don't want you hanging out with that person, I've heard about them'—I got that a lot.

Secondary school

"When I was 15, my metabolism slowed down and I was really worried because I wouldn't be the thing that I always was"

When Sally noticed that her body was changing, she started exercising and dieting to avoid losing the value she had, because being tall was only okay if she was also thin.

> I remember seeing a photo of myself when I was 15 and I had a stomach and I was like, 'You've never had one before' . . . that's the first time that I remember doing something weird with food, like consciously.
>
> I've always just been really anxious about how I look and especially as someone who's tall, it's like, well, you have to look like that. Otherwise, like, what are you doing? You're not beautiful.
>
> People always say that I have really small waist and I think that if I had lost that I would just be huge, I'd just be like a fridge . . . I would be such a hulking person.

"It's this whole neoliberal framework where you have to make the most out of every situation all the time, it's like, why wouldn't you make yourself the best that you can be?"

Thinness for Sally was linked to feminine beauty standards, but it was also associated with personal responsibility for health, something that was demonstrated by her father but which she also recognised in media she consumed.

> It's normal to like, your metabolism slows down and you actually take responsibility for what you eat.
>
> [Dad] he's like 'but you should have seen them, and it's no wonder that they're so unhappy with what they do, because you can tell by their diet'.
>
> I read American Psycho . . . I was like, you know what, he's totally right . . . it should all be about optimisation and making myself the best that it can be . . . I was like, 'If I just try harder, it'll be, I'll fix myself'.

"It's not like you could be friends with kids from other schools"

Sally's cohort had a bully culture, and Sally was often a victim even amongst friends. When Sally was 15, her online diary was unknowingly hacked into by a friend and shared with peers. Sally withdrew further from her peers and her small and isolated community offered little alternatives. Sally's mother organised for Sally to see a therapist.

> They were reading my diary for months. . . . if I spoke to a friend and I felt uncomfortable by it, I would write about it . . . so it was kind of exacerbating all my relationships falling apart . . . everybody that I knew didn't tell me. . . . I couldn't really trust anyone.

I can see bullying happening in Australia, but I can't see it happening to the extent that it did there. Maybe it was because our lives were so small realistically. We only knew a certain amount of people and you couldn't venture past that and [the city] itself was so small. So maybe you did think about all these things so much because it's really all that you had, I only had the ten people that I knew really.

"Beach parties where girls wear their bikinis and go in foam pits, and why did I need to do that as a 15-year-old girl with all these old men?"

The activities shared with peers often exposed and objectified her body, like beach parties and nightclubs. The city afforded the teenagers freedom because there was little crime, little parental supervision and exceptions for white females. With fake ID cards they accessed nightclubs from the age of 16.

We would go to nightclubs, where men who had families bought us drinks . . . girls there are kind of hyper-sexualised . . . girls get in metal cages that would levitate and spin and only hot girls were allowed in . . . ladies night every Wednesday night where girls get free entry and get five free drinks. . . . They would essentially let you in if you were white . . . me and my sister snuck out a lot. . . . We would have been wearing body-con dresses with heels that were 'this big'. . . . Men started to notice me maybe when I was like 14–15 when I think I started wearing different kinds of dresses and things.

"I hate that my self worth was determined by what others did or like could do to me and whether they thought I was beautiful"

Sally began to wear different clothes and grow her hair long to enhance her femininity, which was shaped by what was desirable by males. Sally slept with male friends to get a boyfriend, but it did not eventuate into relationships and gave her peers more reasons to bully her.

I thought that you had to lose your virginity . . . it was what my friends were doing. . . . They all had committed relationships and I think I maybe I just wanted to join in. . . . I needed a boyfriend, I guess. I think that was a narrative that I told myself . . . boys that I was friends with, I would let them sleep with me. . . . I think maybe that's why the bullying kind of happened.

"They all knew that it happened and they would say things to provoke me, like one guy said in front of me, 'girls that are raped ask for it'"

Sally's sister had almost graduated when she was sexually assaulted by a male in Sally's cohort. She told her family and they made a police report, but there was not enough evidence to go to court. The family of the accused male sent defensive letters to the school community, and the students gossiped, calling the family liars or victim blaming. After graduation, Sally's sister escaped to Australia to live with her maternal relatives.

> *My sister was raped by someone that I went to school with, someone that I was in the same circle of friends as me. . . . He was friends with a lot of the people that I thought were my friends and it made me really uncomfortable because no one talked to me about it. And I felt that I didn't want them to pick a side, like, that's not, I didn't want that. No one could just support me for supporting my sister.*

"Everyone knew everything about my family, it seemed. And there was no escape"

After the sexual assault, Sally's parents monitored their activities more closely and there was a greater entanglement between her family and peer relationships.

> *It was challenging having my mum at my school, and when that happened it felt like everybody knew our business all the time. . . . We had to keep it confidential because it could have impacted the investigation. . . . My mum went up to this girl to say you actually can't talk about this. . . . She bitched about my mum to everyone, and she said that my mum intimidated her.*
>
> *The week after it happened, [my sister] and I went clubbing and my mum and dad were furious . . . concerned about how we'd appear if it went to court. But they were always supportive of us. My mum's not very good about talking about our feelings. And my dad didn't really say much.*

"Mum and dad separated and [sister] left, and it was the hardest year of my high school"

Since her sister's cohort graduated and her sister returned to Australia, Sally was alone to cope with her bullies, school rumours and her parents' separation. Sally's father was having an affair and he moved out with the other woman.

> *I was suicidal. . . . I had no friends. and that's when the eating disorder happened. and I was so unhappy because I didn't know what was going on with my family, and none of my friends knew how to talk to me. . . . It kind of sucked in year 12 when my sister left and all those people left because I didn't really have those friends, but I was studying anyway so it was okay.*

"I just had nothing else to do, so I was like, I established a routine, and I was like 'this will distract me'"

Studying gave Sally an excuse to avoid peers and family, and she filled her time with a routine of studying, calorie counting and exercise. Sally displayed concerning physical symptoms, but nobody was concerned by her behaviour because it was normal to have a workout routine and no one was watching her eating.

I would study for eight hours a day, and then I would go to the gym for two and a half hours, and then I would sleep. And then I would do that every day until my exams. But I think it was a good thing for me because I was so depressed that if I didn't exercise, I think it would have been very bad.

It was so nice to be distracted by academia rather than being bullied . . . gave me a break because I was like, 'You're not being left out, no one's seeing each other'. . . . There wasn't that need to hang out with them all the time, I could just use studying as an excuse. . . . It felt nice to just think about my future, having a fresh start, a clean slate, moving back to [Australia], being with family, and not having to deal with all these people that know so much about me.

It's never an eating disorder if you look healthy, so that my parents were like, it's great that she wants to get stronger, and she's spending so much time [at the gym]. . . . . A lot of my female friends had exercise routines; it wasn't something that we necessarily talked about, but I think we were all aware. . . . Girls that I went to high school with had worse eating disorders than me, so I think comparatively I probably didn't think it was a big deal.

University

"I didn't really think about it for a little bit, but it's always been in the back of my mind"

When her family moved back to Australia, Sally's hope for a fresh start paralleled a lapse in her eating disorder. But Sally faced many barriers to the fresh start she anticipated, and over time she began to restrict, calorie count, excessively exercise, binge and purge.

I would binge when no one was around, and as soon as someone was around, I would stop eating. . . . I'd always get so embarrassed if people saw me eat a lot. . . . When he [partner] left the room . . . I'd go and eat more out of the pot, and at times he would catch me . . . something so uncivilised about it . . . the whole image of me stooping over a pot and eating.

My Greek grandparents . . . they would always tell me that I was too skinny, and that I needed to eat more. . . . I have to pretend that I'm not hungry, but I'm really hungry. . . . I want them to point out that I'm skinny.

I'm totally vegan for environmental reasons and ethical reasons . . . but I think something else that attracts me to it is that it's a rule that I don't have to think about, I limit what I eat but I don't even have to think about it.

"I wanted to take a gap year, but my mum didn't let me"

Sally's mother pressured her into studying journalism at university, which made it difficult for Sally to establish a stable independent income. Sally was ineligible to receive study payments from the government because of her parents' pending divorce, and she relied on her relatives to support her. Sally worked casual jobs in hospitality, retail and nightlife, but most of her labour went into unpaid intern-ships to build a portfolio for journalism.

> [Mum] *She's super driven by academia . . . so for my mum to think that my status slipped . . . she was like, 'You have to enrol, my daughter is not working part time at coles'. . . . She was worried that I was going to be doing it long term and not set-tling into a future because she was like, 'Nobody knows what they want to do, but you have to do something'.*
>
> *It was really stressful because with my degree I had to do a lot of internships . . . it was what needed to be done for me to get a job, and that's what I'd heard from everyone. . . . I was just doing a lot of extra stuff because I had to do it from my career, which meant that I couldn't work, so I had no money.*

"I stayed with my dad, even though I wasn't keen on it, but I just had nowhere else to live"

Her maternal relatives accommodated her mother and sister, but Sally moved in with her father which was farther from the city and isolating without private transport and a licence.

> *I stayed with my auntie for a little bit as well, but it was just a bit hectic living there, because I was sharing a room with [sister]. . . . Mum didn't want me to go and stay with my dad because she remembers living in the hills with him and feeling really trapped. . . . I knew that it wasn't good, but I was like I can put up with it if I get a room.*
>
> *Moving to [Australia] was a culture shock. . . . I was missing I guess my life and I was a bit lonely. . . . I was really excited to make a new name for myself and rebrand myself. . . . I didn't make any friends at uni, I was kind of wishing, I was hoping that this would be my clean break and my fresh start, but it didn't happen at uni.*

"I came back and it was really bad living with him, and then I had to move. But that's it, I think the eating, like that's when the eating got bad again"

Sally was homesick so she joined her father on a trip overseas, and on the plane her father got drunk and publicly abused her. When they returned home, Sally's father evicted her and she returned to live with her maternal relatives, where she had a depressive period.

> *We go on the plane, and he gets drunk and he starts abusing me in front of every-one . . . got so bad that other people on the plane had to tell him to stop . . . and the air hostesses had to take me into the cockpit . . . and that was the saddest I've ever been. I threw up because I was so sad.*
>
> *My dad threw me out . . . after the plane incident, because I was ignoring him . . . so I moved back in with my mum and my grandparents, so shared a room*

with my mum. But my mental health was really bad, I was not getting out of bed, I wasn't eating, and I watched the whole Sopranos in two weeks.

"I've always been friends with people that have had eating disorders"

Since her sister had returned a year earlier, she introduced Sally to friends, but they shared eating disorder behaviours. Sally made superficial friends through university, and one showed her a phone app which exacerbated her disorder greatly.

> [Sister] *She's always made friends easier than me. She's really outgoing, and she's really charismatic and she would always let me hang out with her friends.*
>
> *A lot of the girls were really thin, and they were going to the gym, and I have no doubt that they had eating disorders because they were so thin. I just wanted to be thin like them, I wanted to be beautiful and thin like them. . . . I never got as bad as them, one of them smoked meth. It made her really thin, and that's why she did it.*
>
> *He [a university friend] showed me a calorie counting app and that's when I went truly insane with what I ate. And that was the worst thing that ever happened to me.*

Towards recovery

"I think it just stopped becoming so severe"

Sally was never formally diagnosed or treated for her eating disorder, but she achieved a phase of recovery as her behaviours changed alongside changes in her relationships. Sally did go to therapy and although she never spoke to them about her disorder, she only spoke to them about other bad behaviours like drinking and drug-taking.

> *I was in that mindset, I was like, 'I'm not going to talk to you about it, because as soon as I address it, I'll have to do something about it, and I don't want to do anything about it, because I like it. . . . I've never talked to my psychiatrists about my eating disorders really, or my exercise, they've just encouraged me to exercise . . . the psychiatrist and she was like, I don't think you should be drinking . . . I don't think you're mentally well enough. . . . She also told me to not do drugs, so I stopped doing that.*

"I've told my therapist all the abuse that he's put me through, and she said that you need to give him an ultimatum"

Sally's mother paid for Sally to see a therapist again, and she encouraged Sally to assert boundaries with her father. When her father refused to seek support, Sally stopped talking to him for three years but they eventually reconciled and he continued to be a source of stress.

She was like, 'Essentially what he did to you is almost unforgivable unless he seeks help'. . . . I understand that that thinking is a little bit dangerous because it's not that he's choosing to be drunk to hurt me. He's getting drunk because he's dealing with his own mental health issues. But I think when push comes to shove, you have to listen to your family . . . you need to take responsibility.

It was such a bizarre feeling, realising that I didn't love my dad. It felt like I was grieving him but, I don't know, it was kind of also nice. I was taking care of myself, it felt good to do that. . . . I can't actually remember how we reconciled. My dad always comes to my family events because his family don't like him . . . maybe it happened that way . . . [sisters] we never not talk to him at the same time, it's always crazy guilt, we feel that we need to give him affection. Maybe she had a fight with him and I was like, 'I will let him back into my life'.

"That's when we felt like things were turning around and we felt, I don't know, settled"

Sally's mother, who was enjoying the missed proximity to her relatives, was not rushed to move out. But her therapist encouraged her to rent somewhere for herself and her daughters. The relationship between the sisters and their mother strengthened through the separation and learning to talk through therapy.

[My sister] is my best friend now and it's been like that since I was probably like 20 or 19. . . . My mother, my sister went through a lot of therapy and we all have the skills now to identify mental health issues and talk about it . . . was kind of our job to take care of mum a little bit but that's different from taking care of my dad . . . she's the parent that raised us essentially, she's a powerhouse of a woman.

"He kind of restored my faith in men and people in general"

Sally met her now long-term boyfriend, and integrated into his friendship group within a live music and club scene. Sally had belonging and freedom in this scene centred around culture and parties. Although the females in the group were thin and Sally wanted to fit in, she also wanted to be interesting, so she stopped attending the gym religiously to make time for reading, music and movies.

He was the first guy that's never been an asshole to me . . . I felt really respected. And he introduced me to all of his friends . . . they had my back and that was so nice considering my people that I went to high school with, they made fun of me to my face.

I realised that my life had become the gym, and I was boring and all I could talk about was the gym and I just didn't want that for myself. I was like 'You love to read, you love to see your friends and your family, and watch movies', and I was just depriving myself.

While I stopped working out, I rode my bike everywhere . . . when me and [partner] first started dating, that's when I got my bicycle and that was me exercising for fun. . . . It gave me more time for myself which I wanted, but I still wanted to lose weight which is not, probably not good, but I felt like a step in the right direction.

"I told him this as well, that 'I think you're the reason that I kicked the worst parts of my eating disorder'"

Sally and her partner were vegan, but he was a foodie. He took Sally out to eat, cooked for her and *talked a lot* about food as pleasure and exploration. A turning point in Sally's recovery was an overseas trip together. With support from Sally's therapist, she received a back pay of unreceived study allowance, and could afford months of travel. Sally was not able to sustain her eating disorder behaviours in the presence of her partner for this long.

> *I have no excuse not to eat what he's eating. . . . He'd be like, 'I know you forgot to pack lunch today, I'm gonna go drop off some food for you'. . . . We would go out to restaurants all the time and he'd order for me . . . introduced food into my diet that I was actually excited about. . . . He would talk to me about food and I would pay attention to what I put in my mouth. And I learned to love food because he was so in love with food. And I wonder what would have happened if I dated someone who didn't like food, it could have ended really differently.*

Sally learnt to accept some weight–gain because her partner was accepting. Over time Sally was able to talk to her partner about her body concerns and tell him what was helpful and unhelpful.

> *Maybe I felt more loved and it was okay to eat more. Because naturally when I first started dating him I put on a lot of weight because I was starving myself for such a long time . . . he still loved me, so I think that made me feel more comfortable within myself, and I just felt like yeah he actually cared.*
>
> *I've told him that I don't want him to compliment my body, it's not healthy for him to tell me that I look thin or fat, or he's not to say that I look good, that my body looks good at a certain weight. He's very aware of that.*

"Shifted the focus away from food and exercise to my career, but still the habits were not healthy around that either"

After graduation, Sally moved interstate to get hired by the media company she was freelancing for, but this never eventuated. The media company failed to protect the anonymity of a piece she wrote about her father, which introduced a lot of stress, and resulted in her doing more drugs. Working in retail and partying with friends made Sally anxious about her lack of productivity and growth.

> *I'd stopped focusing so much on food, and I started focusing on what did I want to do with my career? . . . I love to make the most of everything and I love to be the best that I can . . . but my problem is just being, I can't just be, I have to think 50 steps ahead about why this activity will serve me.*

I could study and work in a shop or something, I just have to do something that gives me value and I don't think I was doing that [interstate] . . . working in the shop it was really boring. . . . I just wanted a job in my field, and I wanted to be respected enough to be given a job. . . . I've been writing for you guys for years, and you don't think I'm ready for a job? . . . Nobody wants to hire me, I'm not a good journalist, I just felt like I wasn't worth anything.

That stuff with [media outlet] happened and my dad and I just like that I started doing a lot of drugs again . . . I was worried that he [dad] was going to kill himself . . . then I was mad at him for minimising my experience and him saying that's not how it happened.

Recovery

"I feel like the worst is behind me . . . I'm definitely not as bad as I used to be"

Sally continued to have fat-phobic thoughts but challenged them. She habitually approached low calorie meals, but no longer purged or felt shame after eating. She exercised daily, but for stress reduction, pleasure, social connection and strength rather than compensating for calories. Sally was well-read about mental health and eating disorders and was constantly negotiating what was disordered.

My definition of an eating disorder now is totally wack. And I've talked to my sister about it . . . we're not going [to the gym] as much as we used to, and we're doing it for different reasons, but I think we're substituting one ideal of our bodies with another. We wanted to be thin before and we don't now, her and I both want to be, I want to be strong.

Because I've had some kind of eating disorder for ten years . . . I'm worried now that it's not even something that I'm consciously doing. It's just behaviours that are so buried in my head . . . it's not even a decision that I'm making. It's just something that is happening, that I'm not even thinking about.

"Kind of sucked coming back because I felt like I was moving backwards. But in my career I was moving forwards, which is important"

Sally successfully interned overseas for a month at a well-known media outlet, which gave her credibility to find a job back home. Sally won a cadetship in her family's state, and she accepted the position but had mixed feelings about being close to her family.

I was publishing more than both of the other interns combined . . . I was like, 'Hey, you know what, maybe I'm not shit, and I am good at what I can do, maybe they just weren't giving me the platform to do it'.

My mum really coddled me and that's why I wanted to go [interstate]. I really liked the independence, I was like, I'm doing what I want to do, I'm on my own, I'm

living with like some friends. . . . I think that's why I'm not thrilled about being back
here . . . most journalists have to move anyway and at least I got to move home . . .
I really missed my mum, my sister, my grandparents.

[Grandparents] they love us no matter what we're doing . . . they've always been
there. . . . I think that they're doing what my dad should have done. . . . They're
70-year-old Greeks who lived through World War Two . . . they've never done
therapy, and it's crazy that they managed to understand and support us.

"I don't have a life. I work all the time. That's probably my biggest problem right now"

The news cycle made deadlines stressful, and her role was insecure and under-
paid. But Sally accepted these conditions because the opportunities were limited, especially in writing the stories which gave Sally 'meaning'. She put in
extra hours to protect her position and compete against others, which came at
a sacrifice to her social life.

I get a lot of value out of my job because there is this justice element to it. . . . I think
that once I lose that, then I won't want to do it. I don't know what else I can really
do, I kind of have to do this job.

I'm a graduate from uni and I currently only get paid $90 more than 'job
keeper' . . . the recession will make jobs like mine really scarce. I know of lots of
people that have been laid off. So I think the fact that I still have a job is something
I should probably hang on to.

"I don't need to be a serious journo all the time. And I need just take a break from it sometimes"

Sally's eating disorder behaviours produced meanings of femininity that she
shared with her sister and friends, providing Sally with play and fun. Her thinness was a point of difference amongst friends where Sally did not consider
herself funny or charming enough to win attention.

I was spending a lot of time with my work friends, but . . . they don't need to be my
whole life because they kind of are anyway . . . we are all super serious people . . .
and I don't need to talk about that all the time. I need to hang out with, my sister
vetoes me whenever I talk about that stuff and that's good . . . I need to talk about
people and trends and dumb fashions and lip filler.

I don't think that I'm funny, and I don't think, I think that I'm smart, but
I think that what I've always been is tall and thin, and I wouldn't want them to not
think that I'm tall and thin anymore. So I think it is, it is my friends and my family.

When my sister gets funny about her body, I do as well. I've noticed that started
happening now, she's working out all the time and she's doing intermittent fasting,
and now that I know that she's doing that, I feel I'm competitive.

I cannot wait [for the pandemic to end] I'm actually shopping now for the sluttiest
dress that I can find, so I can look really good when this is all over.

Male attention helped construct their shared femininity, but Sally did not experience influence over men through her femininity, instead relying on her knowledge and verbal skills to dominate them.

> *I always get paranoid that my male friends don't like me . . . the female friends that I'm with, definitely in men's eyes have more value . . . I could never ensnare a man like other women can . . . I am confident that I can talk politics with them . . . I want to be able to be equal to a man, I want to terrify them by the way that I talk . . . they've always managed to make me feel shit, so I want to be smarter.*

Journalism provided an identity that was in some ways protective against her eating disorder. But she still thought about her body to avoid appearing too feminine or sexualised and not being taken seriously by her male colleagues.

> *I don't want to be sexualised at work . . . I've got this paranoia of my male colleagues thinking that I'm a slut and I'm not smart enough . . . that's why I don't wear skirts to work, or high heels . . . but it's such cognitive dissonance because I work so hard on my image, and then I'm like 'don't look at me'.*

"Those issues that I had growing up persisted. But I think because I had friends that supported me and I wasn't living with him, that I was able to deal with him better"

Once Sally's parents stopped sustaining a friendship and officially divorced, the sisters could limit contact with their father further. His behaviour continued to turn abusive, but it was easier when they united against him.

> *When things do hit the fan with my dad, I do get anxious. . . . I blocked his number, but then I just started like crying and shaking, and I was worried that he was going to come to my house . . . my housemate kind of had to talk me down, but that day I hadn't eaten anything now that I think about it.*
>
> *He lives so far away, and our lives don't cross over at all . . . me and my sister just decided that we needed to do therapy with him. . . . I feel so much better not having him in my life. I kind of want this to be the final try, if this doesn't work, then I don't really want to do it anymore.*

"He's really good, he never, he just wants what I want, which is cool"

Sally's partner moved back with her, and his encouragement to enjoy life was important to her recovery, as was the influence he afforded her in the relationship.

> *He's really supportive. I think he would make a really good dad, that's the only reason why I'd want to have kids . . . but I've told him that if it happens, I'm not giving up my career, and he has to stay home and take care of them. And he said, 'Yeah, that's fine'. And I was like, 'Cool, you've made it so easy for me'.*

"I've got a rainy day fund, which is enough for me to move overseas and start a new life"

Although Sally's relatives were an important source of support, she got comfort from saving enough money to travel overseas whenever she wanted.

> *I've managed to save up a lot of money in case I want to leave. . . . So I'm really happy with myself that I've done that, but that's kind of the first time I've ever been able to do that.*

11 Fiona's story

The weight of expectations

Beyond the way that her body looked, Fiona emphasised the need for eating small amounts to preserve financial resources. Even when money was no longer a big issue for her family, Fiona's habit of eating small portions remained as she was reluctant to lose the frame and thinness that she had been praised for. After discovering exercise and the validation this provided, Fiona's disordered behaviour increased. The rest of her experience was peppered with attempting to avoid being burdensome to her parents, manage an abusive relationship and navigate early adulthood. When she was diagnosed with anorexia nervosa, she was reluctant to accept this diagnosis. She did not think she was 'sick enough' and had rigid ideas about what someone with an eating disorder looked like. Her recovery has not been a linear journey, but Fiona has spoken positively about the lessons she has learnt through her experiences.

Childhood

Fiona attributes some of her early eating disorder thoughts around needing to be the best, to feelings of loneliness at home and at school. Fiona was more anxious, sensitive and teary than her siblings. At school she was "ugly" because she had glasses and did not get attention from male peers.

I'm one of four kids. I have two brothers and one sister. I'm the eldest daughter. I just grew up with them and my parents.

Ever since a young age, I always felt like I had to be the best. I was a very anxious child. I was always crying and always scared of something going wrong or something happening. Or just, I would just overreact to the most mundane things. Yeah, I was just always known as the crier. I couldn't control my emotions. I didn't want to be that way. I didn't want to be the crier. I didn't want to be anxious, but I couldn't help it. At the time I didn't even have the language to explain what was going on. I was what, 8 or 9, and I didn't know what anxiety was so I couldn't explain what I was feeling.

I started to hate myself. I noticed that I was different to other kids and that they might treat me differently because of how I acted. Which makes sense now. But at

DOI: 10.4324/9781003453918-13

the time it just made me feel worse because I felt like no one understood me and I had no one to turn to, I guess. It made me feel really alone.

I was objectively an ugly kid. I had glasses. I looked different to other kids. And I didn't look how I wanted to look. And I knew that boys didn't find me attractive. I knew boys didn't have crushes on me. And I guess that kind of contributed to my self-esteem issues as well. I knew that boys weren't interested in me. I knew who the pretty girls at school were, and who the ugly girls at school were.

I just grew up that way. I was just always worried about what people were thinking of me, how people perceived me, whether or not people liked me. I guess because I knew that they didn't, but I didn't know how to change that or change myself to get people to like me.

Even though I had friends, I had this sense, that now I know it was anxiety or whatever, but at the time I just, I always thought that all my friends were just pretending to like me. Or that everyone secretly hated me but no one was telling that to my face. And that they must be talking about me behind my back so I thought I would be so stupid to not see that. That's such a strange thing for a child to experience like, now, in hindsight, I think that your childhood should just be such a happy and carefree time. But I was just always so worried about things. And I think a lot of that came from just how I grew up and what I was around.

Fiona missed out on support as she was not able to communicate how she was feeling to those around her, because she did not have the language but also because of the mental health 'stigma' in the family, and their lack of response to her emotions.

There was a lot of stigma about mental health in my family so I hadn't learnt what that meant or that I could talk about it. . . . I couldn't articulate what I was experiencing because no one had spoken about that around me.

I didn't get the support that I needed, which I've come to realise now. But at the time I didn't, I was just a child, so I wasn't going to reach out for support myself. I needed someone to be the adult and I needed someone to take care of me or I needed someone to say, I don't know, get me to speak to someone about it or get someone to help.

Besides Fiona's difficulties regarding social relationships, she also had challenges growing up in a poor family.

My family was quite poor growing up, we didn't have a lot of money. And I feel like my brothers really didn't worry about that type of stuff. But I was always so worried about money, always worried about my parents spending money, and whether we were going to have enough money and not wanting them to spend money on me because they didn't have a lot. And I guess I was so worried about everything that is not within a child's control . . . I don't think that's something that a kid should have to stress about. But I did stress about it.

And because I was always thinking about money and stuff like that I would pay attention to how my mum spoke about money. We would have to obviously budget and think about how much food we'd buy and being quite, I don't know if diligent is the right word. But just paying attention to what we made and not wasting food is what I'm trying to say. So we'll just basically make enough for everyone to eat. And that would normally mean that I would have the least amount of food and never really thought about it growing up.

Eating small amounts was normalised for Fiona during her childhood due to lack of resources. Although she suspects this alone did not lead to restrictive eating later on, she thinks it was one of many factors which combined to create these habits.

I don't think I necessarily had to eat as much as some others to feel full. I wasn't the kid that had to eat a lot, unlike my brothers. So I didn't really think about it. . . . It wasn't weird to me how little I was eating. But because of that I'd grown up really thin. Petite, skinny, whatever you want to call it, I was just small. . . . So if I think about it, it wasn't about caring about the calories or the quality of the food or whatever, it was about eating less to save money.

As an adult, Fiona felt angry that she was expected to help her mother as she was the eldest daughter. Her brothers did not have the same experiences with financial-related stress or have to care for their young sister.

I was always the caregiver, not the one being given care. . . . A kid shouldn't have to sacrifice our own well-being to help others.

At the time, Fiona did not see a problem with the responsibilities given to her. She thought that if she was helpful enough, she would be loved and cared for. At the time, her brother was diagnosed with a mental disorder and she avoided exacerbating the family's stress and being a burden.

I needed to be known as the helpful one, I needed to be known as the good child, just so badly wanted to be thanked or praised or given this positive attention. But it was the attention that I wasn't given. Because I was always fine just doing things and I never really said no. So it was just expected of me.

Fiona had a close relationship with her grandmother, who would not leave the house until she deemed herself presentable enough to be seen in public. She would often make remarks towards Fiona about how it was necessary to make good impressions on people through your appearance. Most of Fiona's grandmother's body talk was directed at herself; she would also praise Fiona for being thin. These remarks about the value of thinness from her grandmother, who gave her so much attention, influenced Fiona's behaviour going forward.

My grandma was always so verbally conscious of how she looked. And I think that was so unhealthy for a young girl to be absorbing. She was constantly body checking, and doing it out loud as well, just talking about how ugly she looked that day, or how fat she was, or how she needed to lose weight. . . . If we were ever eating together, she wouldn't eat, or she would eat very little. And like at the time, I just thought that was normal for her.

I was very close to my grandma while I was growing up. Seeing your role model talk down on themselves constantly like that, all the time, starts to affect you. . . . In the end, she has reasons for why she acted like that and spoke like that. But I just don't think that you should talk about your body like that in front of a young child, a young, impressionable girl.

Maybe I just started comparing myself to everyone because she put that dialogue in my head. That dialogue of hating yourself and wanting to change and not being beautiful. And fat being a bad thing.

Secondary school

Fiona did not know much about eating disorders when her own started to emerge in high school. From watching movies, she assumed people with eating disorders were only in hospitals.

When my eating disorder first started, I didn't even know that I had an eating disorder, because I was used to eating not much growing up. . . . So the behaviours and thoughts might have been there from when I was, I don't know, 14 or so.

It would sort of come in waves, I mean the thoughts about my body were there quite frequently when I was that age, and I would occasionally be like, Oh, I won't eat this, because of this reason. But it wasn't so regular.

When Fiona's body-image thoughts emerged at 14 years old, she experienced many transitions: starting high school, new peers, puberty, conversations about bodies and changing roles at home. The most important thing to Fiona was how she looked to other people, particularly male peers.

I had always compared my body to other people's and that, but I didn't really do anything about it. Because I was naturally skinny, I also didn't know what to do about it, I didn't think about all these different ways or ways to lose weight. But I did always compare my body.

All I cared about was what other people thought. I would walk through school, wondering whether anyone was looking at me. If they were, what were they thinking of me? I was sitting in class, what are people thinking about? Are they thinking about me today? Do I look bad today? How do I want people to perceive me? That's what my whole world revolved around, how I wanted to be perceived.

It wasn't until about year nine where I kind of got out of that awkward stage. But guys still weren't really paying attention to me. I hate to say it, but all I was looking for was male validation. That's all the girls at high school would talk about: who has a crush on who, who's dating who? This girl is so pretty, this girl isn't.

Fiona tried to manage her family's expectations with her peer's expectations. She didn't have the money to buy things that her peers thought were cool, or to attend events that the popular kids were. She described trying her best to make everything appear normal, and to hide her efforts to fit in.

> *I think that's the saddest part. I didn't care if I was smart, I wanted people to think I was smart. I didn't care if I was pretty, I wanted people to think that I was pretty. I didn't care if I was cool, I wanted people to think that I was cool.*

Meeting her family's expectations did not sustain attention and praise for long, so she worked harder to exceed expectations. Fiona had always eaten little portions, but she started to play a game with herself and see how long she could go without eating. Despite always being thin and eating little, Fiona began to exercise excessively and weigh herself.

> *I always wanted that attention, I just wanted praise, and when it comes down to it I basically just wanted to be loved, really, I just wanted someone to care about me. And logically I know that there's people out there that care about me, I know my parents care about me, but it wasn't given the way that I wanted it to be. And it wasn't showed as much as it maybe should have been.*
>
> *I didn't even notice really that I was losing weight. Sometimes I realised that I hadn't eaten in a few days. And I'd have this sense of pride that I hadn't eaten. Even though I wasn't telling anyone about it. I'd kind of just make it a competition with myself. Like, let's see how long I can go without eating this time or how little I can eat.*
>
> *I was always the one getting good grades and that just became the normal for me, so I stopped getting that praise. And what I did felt never good enough for my parents or my family. So I would just keep trying harder and harder. And I guess that manifested into my eating disorder. Because the weight was like, what I look like was never good enough, how much I weighed was never good enough. I've always had to exercise more, eat less, look better, work harder. And it was so unhealthy.*

When a new boy moved to Fiona's school, she saw this as an opportunity to attract the male attention that she was seeking.

> *When I met the boy that became my first boyfriend and he showed interest in me, I was just dumbstruck. I thought that because this boy showed interest in me, that he must be the only boy that thought I was pretty or liked me.*

Fiona's expectations of her high school boyfriend were influenced by the conversations with many family members. In her family, it was the norm to get married very young to the first person you dated. Fiona was a "naïve" teenager, and put this expectation on her first boyfriend despite there being issues in the relationship.

> *In hindsight, he was very manipulative. But at the time, I thought he was just this golden boy, that he was so in love with me, and we would be together forever. Because basically all of my family married their high school sweetheart. And in my head,*

I had this idea that I had to also marry the person that I dated in high school. So I think that's one of the reasons that I stayed with him for so long.

I wasn't even sure I liked him that much to begin with. But I convinced myself I did because I was insecure. And he kind of just changed his behaviour to appeal to me. Later, I discovered that it wasn't the real him. He was changing the way that he acted so that I would like him.

When her boyfriend's behaviour turned emotionally abusive, Fiona did not talk to anyone about what was going on and she stayed in the relationship to avoid disappointing or upsetting anyone. She had few other friends in relationships that she could speak to or compare with.

Things just got out of hand. When I would try to break up with him, he wouldn't let me, or he would rope me into staying with him. Somehow, he would really guilt trip me. Sometimes he would say he wanted to kill himself. If I broke up with him, he'd hurt himself. Or he would do something so bad to hurt me. And then he would say that he's so in love with me. He's so sorry, and blah, blah, blah.

Later on down the track that turned into 'No one else will love you' and 'If you leave me no one else is going to find you attractive. You're crazy. Do you really think that anyone else would put up with you besides me?' Or it would be 'We've been together for so long, why would you waste these years and break up with me?'

Since that was my first relationship, and I was young and I was impressionable, I couldn't see whether this was right or wrong. Most of my friends weren't in relationships at this stage. So I couldn't compare it to my friends' relationships.

Without the knowledge of what emotional abuse looked like, Fiona listened to her partner and blamed herself. Fiona's eating disorder behaviour increased, and she would talk to her boyfriend about it, but he would encourage her not to eat. Fiona tried to break up with her boyfriend, but he did not let her. She lost friends because her boyfriend spread rumours about her, and this could get worse if she broke up with him.

I couldn't understand what had changed or what I'd done wrong. So I thought it must have been something wrong with me. He was the person I had confided the most in about my eating disorder, and he would literally encourage it. I would say something along the lines of, 'Oh god, I really don't want to eat today. I look so fat, I hate myself so much', and he would reply, 'Just don't eat then'. In hindsight, clearly that is a deranged thing to say to someone with anorexia. At the time, though, I was looking for anything to excuse or justify my behaviour. So my eating disorder would love when he would say stuff like that because it encouraged me to keep going. He told me that if I gained weight, he would break up with me.

I would try to break up with him all the time. I resented him, actually I think I just straight up hated him sometimes while we were dating. But at the same time, I didn't want him to be the one to break up with me. Because I wanted to break up with him, and he wouldn't let me. So I didn't want him to go around and tell everyone that he broke up with me and spread rumours about me. He had already spread other rumours about me while I was in high school and made me lose so many friends that I knew that if we broke up, then he would just create more rumours or say other things about me or just I don't even know what exactly I was afraid of.

Graduation and going to the gym

After high school, Fiona started going to the gym regularly. She had never been athletic but the people she admired online were, so she tried it herself. Regular gym–goers would notice her and talk to her, and she got attention inside and outside of the gym for the hours she put in to working out.

> *I started going to a gym, where there was group fitness classes. And it became my competitive nature coming out again. It's hard to explain because I actually don't think I'm competitive. I just think I'm competitive with myself.*
>
> *I think it was the nature of this gym as well, I loved going there. And there was this social aspect as well. But it was like, you're almost rewarded based on how many classes you attended. Not rewarded with something tangible or anything but people would notice if you were there a lot, because it was the same sort of people that are going around, and people will make comments, and it was good. It was praise. And I think that's what I was lacking, was praise at that time.*
>
> *People, they'd make comments on how fit I was, and 'Oh my gosh, I couldn't do that'. They would praise me, and I would feed off of that. The more I went, the more that people noticed.*

Although Fiona said she was exercising from the praise of attending the gym rather than weight-loss, she still had critical thoughts about her body being too 'fat'.

> *But I just wanted to be skinny, I wanted to have abs, I wanted to look like the people on Instagram. Sometimes I would sit there and just compare myself to photos on Instagram for hours. It makes me sick to think about the amount of time I spent doing that.*
>
> *I had a locked folder on my phone of photos of my body which were intended as the 'before', so that when I lost the amount of weight I wanted to, or was finally satisfied with my body, I could compare it with an 'after' photo. I don't think I could have ever been satisfied with my body, no matter how much weight I lost or how I looked.*
>
> *I was looking in the mirror and I thought I was huge when I was so skinny. . . . Even when I was at my skinniest, I still didn't think I was skinny. . . . I would look in the mirror and I would hate myself, no matter what I looked like.*

Fiona recognised, even at the time, that she may never be happy with the way that she looked. Rather than seeing that as a problem to be addressed, she saw it as a challenge to see how far she could push herself. She spent all her free time outside of university classes and work at the gym, with little left over except to sleep.

I had to work out every day . . . I just did it without question. . . . If I missed a day, I would literally just have a mental breakdown. I would just feel so anxious, I would cry, I would be so irritable. Just because I missed exercising for one day.

With eating very little and exercise for hours a day, that's just obviously not enough to fuel my body. . . . I felt so tired all the time. Sometimes I'd literally just be so drowsy, like falling asleep in the middle of an exercise in class. I couldn't see what was wrong with that.

Therapy

Her emotionally abusive relationship was the reason Fiona made an appointment to see a psychologist. She completed an intake questionnaire before her first appointment, which included questions about eating and exercising behaviour, and a psychologist specialising in eating disorders contacted her to arrange an appointment. She was shocked to be diagnosed with anorexia nervosa.

I was unaware that I had an eating disorder, I actually didn't even know that I had one until I went to a psychologist because of my anxiety. I was just in general having a really bad time in life. And I wanted to speak to someone about it, because things were getting quite bad for me in the relationship and other reasons. And I guess they noticed that I might have had some problems with eating and exercising. And then they referred me to see a psychologist that specialised in eating disorders. And they diagnosed me with anorexia, which I was just completely unaware of. I remember being so confused because how do you even have an eating disorder and not even know it?

I don't even think that I had a real mental picture of what I looked like. My mind was so distorted, that I just couldn't even tell. I couldn't describe myself, like one of the activities I had to do in therapy was to just talk about my body neutrally . . . I just had no concept of what I looked like.

Due to Fiona's idea of eating disorders requiring hospitalisation, she did not initially agree with the psychologist's diagnosis. Despite downplaying her symptoms, her psychologist would still point out behaviours and patterns as being 'disordered'. Fiona began to consider her diagnosis after being made to talk about weight and weigh herself, and experiencing the distress that came with this. After a couple of sessions, Fiona accepted that she had an eating disorder.

And I guess that kind of changed how the treatment went. Because I didn't recognise it for myself. So I was kind of in denial for a bit or I would compare it to other people. Mine wasn't as bad as theirs, or mine can't be that bad, because I'm not this way, or whatever. But as treatment went on, and I was kind of exposed to things I was uncomfortable with, that I didn't even realise I was uncomfortable with, and as we started talking about different topics that I had avoided, I realised that I was avoiding them.

But because I didn't know if I was consciously avoiding the topics or not, like weight-gain and stuff like that. . . . Of course, I didn't want to gain weight. But

I didn't know that I would have such an aversion to seeing the number on the scale change. So I think that's what was difficult for me, was just not knowing what I was uncomfortable with until I was confronted with it.

Her psychologist asked her to talk with family about what was going on, but Fiona rejected the idea and avoided damaging her reputation as a good daughter who didn't cause trouble.

The few times the psychologist tried to get me to open up and get me to tell my family, I couldn't. I didn't have it in me to tell them, I didn't want to disappoint them. I didn't want them to worry about me, because I already had so much going on there we'd already had so much to worry about.

I didn't want anyone to worry about me. I just wanted people to be happy. And I thought that if they knew what I was going through that they would be disappointed in me. And I couldn't have that because I wasn't the disappointment, I had to make everyone proud.

I based my worth on being the best. Making my family proud, making them happy, I could never disappoint them. So I didn't even tell them, my family still don't know that I even had an eating disorder.

Recovery

Fiona's recovery followed the end of the relationship with her abusive boyfriend. She was able to end the relationship now because she had made new close friendships. Without the competing abusive discourses of her boyfriend, Fiona was able to engage in the discourse of therapy and find new ways to talk about herself.

I realised who [ex-boyfriend] said I was and who I really am were two completely different people. . . . I don't know why I put up with how I was treated for so many years, but it was like an epiphany I had one day that I could leave him, that he couldn't force me to stay with him. . . . It was really scary, but it was the greatest form of self-care I ever did.

When Fiona eventually initiated a new romantic relationship, not only was her new relationship free from abuse, but her partner understood her eating disorder because he had a family member previously diagnosed with anorexia.

When I started dating my new boyfriend, I realised how messed up my ex was. [New boyfriend] helped me regain my relationship with food and have a more balanced world-view in general.

Fiona's bad family situation was not addressed through therapeutic intervention. In fact, she avoided talking about anything non-eating disorder related while in therapy. Although her eating disorder behaviours were reduced, many elements of her distress were unaddressed. For now, she was enjoying her new and improved partnership and friendships. But she did consider addressing her family situation in the future.

> *I still haven't told my family, but it's something I think I could be prepared to do in the future. For now, my relationship with food is better than it has ever been. I have great friends, a great partner . . . it's almost like the blind-fold that my eating disorder had on me has been lifted and I'm seeing clearly for the first time.*

12 Courtney's story

Out of the frying pan into the fire

Courtney had the perfect childhood, until changes in the family dynamics meant she needed an "escape". In escaping her homelife, she was faced with negative body-image discourse and unusual eating behaviours. Her unusual eating behaviours fluctuated over time as her contexts changed, something she began to understand as a "domino effect".

> I've never seen all of these different things in my life as a bit of a domino effect . . . sexual assault . . . experiences with my neighbours . . . my mum's mental health, my dad's absence . . . my shitty family . . . their obsessions with crash dieting and body-image . . . and then out of nowhere . . . BAM, 'Oh my God, everything is connected'.

Perfect childhood

Courtney was raised in a country town outside of Adelaide, with her sister who is five years younger than her, and her two parents. Her mother came from a conservative English family, and her father from a Greek Pentecostal Christian family. Growing up, her father was a minister at the church that the extended family attended and her mother was her role model. She recalls her mother was extremely supportive of her and would perform quintessential "homely" tasks such as cooking, cleaning and gardening.

> My very earliest memories of mum were, I always saw her as like obsessed with clean, like everything smelled like bleach, you know, but you know, loved her gardening, always with a big straw hat, you know, all the cooking and, you know, she was a heavy, heavy support for us.
>
> She used to be extremely sporty . . . when she had kids, it wasn't so much sport but she still took us to the beach constantly . . . she was like the perfect role model.

Courtney's extended family also lived in the same town and were fundamentally involved in her childhood. Her grandmothers were particularly salient in the development of her core values and beliefs.

DOI: 10.4324/9781003453918-14

It was probably more my grandmas that influenced any of my . . . 'Don't do this', and, 'You should do that'. Or those types of things.

Mum comes from quite a conservative family. Very, very British. So she was always really concerned and really worried . . . she was always very polite, and I guess, you know, these things just rub off on me.

Nan on my mum's side . . . she was really loving and nice . . . Nan was born in 1922. You know, so I had quite a—It was an old school mentality.

. . . On my dad's side, though, we used to see Nana . . . quite a bit, but she was pretty brutal . . . Nan favouritised . . . my younger cousin, and she didn't really teach me anything other than, 'Sit down, shut up. Don't touch that, [your cousin] might eat it. Don't do this. Don't do that'.

Courtney's paternal family were also obsessed with "looking the part".

They had this obsession with looking the part, because they were poor . . . trying to look like they've got their shit together.

Despite their differences, both sides of the family had a strong relationship with food. They taught Courtney the power of food within a community.

Coming from, not just a Greek family but you know my mum as well, who's English. . . . Like my family, all of them have a pretty strong relationship with food. It's a very 'community' thing, very 'coming together', very important for everyone.

Big changes: "It was so opposite to what I was brought up, not only around, but to believe in"

Her family dynamic shifted, however, when Courtney was around 9 years old and her father began studying science. The nature of his study meant he was often absent, sometimes leaving the country for months at a time.

At the beginning of his career [he was] constantly out of the country for his field research and everything. He was in America, I think at one stage for three months. There was barely any contact.

This meant that her mother became the sole income earner and was left at home with two young children. The lack of support resulted in a substantial decline in her mental well-being. She began to struggle to provide her daughters with the same level of support she had once given them.

When things got really bad [with mum], and that's all we ever saw of her. It was just negative after negative. [She] couldn't make us food, couldn't get out of bed . . . those real debilitating moments.

> *Once mum's depression really set in the house just became a bomb. It was so opposite to what I was brought up, not only around, but to believe in. So that was, that really affected me.*

This change also impacted the extended family, as Courtney's immediate family stopped attending church shortly after her father began studying.

> *We were all brought up Christian. . . . We stopped pretty much going to the church once dad—he used to be trained to be a minister. And then once he was involved in science, that was like, 'Right, off we go'. So we were definitely the black sheep of the family.*

While her father was absent and did not rely on the extended family as much, Courtney was still seeing her father's family. As a result, she faced the burden of the family's departure from the church.

> *I used to actually get bullied within my family quite a bit as well—not my immediate family, my extended . . . their not acceptance of me because I wasn't some goody-two-shoes Christian kid.*

Courtney's extended family on her father's side were also fixated on body-image and presentation. This, alongside leaving the church and losing that connection to her community, made her question her worth.

> *It made me lose that self-worth . . . [my cousins] were all obsessed with their dieting . . . and even just 'godly', which is really hard because I used to be. But then I removed myself. . . . So it's like . . . they were everything that I wasn't, so I obviously came to really resent the church, which then in turn was like resenting them, and them resenting me.*

So, with her father absent, her mother's decline in mental well-being and the loss of community on her father's side, her family unit that she had once cherished and admired, became disjointed. But even when her father was around, it often led to fights between him and her mother.

> *They had that stupid notion in their head of you know, 'The parents need to stay together for kids', and obviously, it was like, 'No . . . you're just harming the family more. You clearly don't love each other'. You know, 'Why is mum sleeping behind . . . the closet?'*

The changes in her parents' relationship towards each other and towards their children encouraged Courtney to step into a parent-like role for her younger sister.

I was very much the 'dad' of the house. I took on very much the father role. I used to look after—my sister's five years younger than me. So, you know, she used to refer to me sometimes as 'mum'.

School

Courtney's school life was difficult as she struggled to maintain relationships with her friends due to her frequent absenteeism.

I used to miss a lot of school with—because of actually tonsillitis of all things. I missed most of year five, which really messed with relationships and social circles. And that's, that's definitely where things went downhill for me. . . .

I used to get . . . bullied a lot in like, but within my friend group, so it wasn't that you could escape to your mates.

This affected Courtney's self-worth and so she refused to attend, resulting in further conflict within her household.

I just lost all of my friends, all my contacts. And then I just didn't want to go to school anymore. And obviously, things kept getting worse with my relationship with my parents as well.

Mum and dad never knew how to deal with me, so they'd like, literally drag me of out of bed by the ankles, they were just exasperated, and they let their emotions run wild and they'd freak out.

Courtney not attending school reflected poorly within her community, and her mother's friends began to bully Courtney about this, something her mother passively allowed.

Mum really did get worse and worse over the years . . . had quite toxic friends that would refer to me as 'bludger'.

She'd just be that quiet person in the background that would allow their children to be bullied, really, by her friends, and they were her escape. So she never stood up to them.

Asking parents for help

Courtney's self-worth was becoming progressively more negative, affecting her mental well-being. She approached her parents about her depressive feelings; however, she quickly wished she had not said anything when they tried to "help" her.

I remember first confessing to feeling depressed . . . and I was literally dragged to the principal's office, and it was so intimidating and I'm sitting there, and there was like this big meeting . . . all these higher up teachers and my parents involved . . . and it's like no one talks to me because they're bloody idiots. And you know it's like things escalate . . . it's all good intention.

Escaping

To escape her homelife, Courtney would often visit the family next door, where her best friend Betty lived. Her behaviours when escaping parental responsibilities were shaped by the way her mother, who had allowed her friends to bully Courtney. Both Courtney and her mother used these behaviours to maintain their "escape" relationships.

I'd constantly disappear next door . . . everyone knew each other in the neighbourhood. So, yeah, we used to just randomly go to people's houses. And yeah, pretty much just escape my parents. . . .

I would do a lot of parental role things, and then I'd rebel in different ways. And a lot of the time at the beginning I'd take things out on [my sister]. Like . . . excluding her from going next door, letting the neighbours pick on her . . . stuff that I regret immensely. . . . I always wanted to stand up for her, and stop these things, but, I think, you know, in my child mind it was kind of like, 'These people are my escape'. . . . I didn't want the responsibility of [my sister] when I went next door.

Betty's family had a perfect image within their community, something that Courtney had lost since her childhood.

They're a very fake family. Lots of people think that they're really community based and loving and you know what I mean, but it's that veneer until you get close to them, which obviously I was extremely close to them.

The family's perfect image was not just about community; they were also obsessed with body-image.

The neighbours were already body-obsessed . . . the mum might come in the room, and she just grabbed her like, not fat, like her skin on her stomach, saying about how she was fat. You know, like exceptionally bad body-image issues.

Betty's family also sexualised Courtney from a young age; however, this family was important to her and so their comments often validated her place within their home.

I was laying there in my bikini on the couch, stinking hot day. And the dad comes in and he was going on about how I looked like a swimsuit model laying there on his couch . . . I would have been-early teens . . . in hindsight, that's creepy as fuck, but then it's kind of like, 'Oh he notices that, like, my body looks good. That is good'.

I remember the dad looking at my photos and going on about, 'Where are the ones with the cleavage?' . . . always drunkenly looking down my top, or if it wasn't him it was . . . the son being a creep in some way. Always belittling but trying it on me. . . . So, I guess trying to pull me down, to kind of weaken me. . . . I really had no confidence as a result of them

Development of unusual eating behaviours

New ways to rebel

At the age of 16, as many teenagers do, Courtney began to gain weight. This negatively impacted her mental health. So, Courtney began to engage in weight-loss behaviours. It was something that she felt pride in but was also a way for her to rebel against her parents.

I remember at one stage, I would just stop eating. . . . I remember losing . . . I think it was five kilos in two weeks. And mum didn't believe me.

. . . In one sense, I was legitimately really happy. Like, I just remember that feeling, like . . . I pulled off something ridiculous. . . . And then on the other side . . . I wanted to freak [mum] out. Then it really pissed me off that she didn't believe me. I remember feeling really upset and angry that she thought that I was a liar.

Fitting into tight roles

When Courtney was 17, her parents separated. While she was not upset about her parents' marriage ending, the change and the tension that came from the separation was distressing for her. Courtney decided to move with her father as her mother's behaviours were not conducive for her mental health. This, however, was upsetting for her younger sister.

Mum and dad broke up when I was about 17 . . . you know, there's drama in that but . . . it was more like the change was crap, not so much them breaking up, because it was good that they broke up . . . so I was living with dad for a bit because I just couldn't cope with mum. She was a hoarder as well. . . . I wasn't coping mentally . . . that heavily affected my sister because she saw it as me abandoning her when obviously I was her only support.

With these changes, Courtney sought further distraction from her neighbours. They introduced laxatives as a way of "cleansing" her body.

[I was] 17 when I started the laxatives. . . . I started going pretty hard . . . then they just stopped working. So, it was like, 'Well, what do I do next?' . . . After the laxatives I'd be at the gym like six days a week with this family next door.

That's how it pretty much started I'd say . . . and I actually got those, like, laxatives from my neighbour . . . going on about how it's cleansing.

Change in behaviour

When Courtney was 18, she had stopped taking laxatives and going to the gym, and had some weight-gain. However, around this time, she had some negative experiences and soon began engaging in bulimia nervosa behaviours.

> *I couldn't do anorexia . . . because I like my food too much . . . so then I went bulimic.*

Sexual assaults

On an interstate trip with Betty, Courtney unfortunately had her first sexual encounter in the form of sexual assault. Her eating disorder behaviours became rampant following this.

> *I ended up getting really drunk and some guy taking advantage of me. And that was actually my first time . . . it was like, 'Okay, I feel crap about myself. I feel dirty', I had to take the morning after pill for the first time. And that's obviously not a nice experience . . . the more I think about it, that's probably when I started with my bulimia.*

A few months later, again when she was out with Betty, she was sexually assaulted.

> *I was actually taken advantage of again, not that long after, when I was at the pub with my neighbour. So that was the second time I'd ever done it . . . so I'd started vomiting all around that.*

At this point, she was beginning to feel a degree of validation from these assaults, as sexualised behaviour was something that became normalised when she visited Betty's family. These sexualised behaviours were then reinforced by her friend Stella who she began spending time with.

> *I was 100% taken advantage of, I was exceptionally drunk. I did not consent, you know, all that crap. But it's like, as messed up as it was, it was like, I was getting attention, like, attention for someone that was always treated so shit. I think that I amped up vomiting, because obviously it had desired effects, or I thought it did. . . . I don't know what my head was doing honestly, I don't even know if it actually did have desired effects . . . and the more I hung out with [Stella]—because she was even more sexualised, than [Betty], if that's even possible. So then, [I became] obsessed with wanting to look good . . . I got to the stage where like, I'd feel ill, if I wasn't vomiting because my stomach obviously wasn't used to having food in it.*

Too far

By the time Courtney was 20, she had been consistently engaging in eating disorder behaviours for several years. She was living with her mother again and was dating a man. Unfortunately, she was again sexually assaulted at a party. This event was much more traumatic than the previous assaults for multiple reasons.

> *The third time happened at a party, and it was really traumatic . . . and then literally the next day, the guy that I was seeing at the time [forced me to have sex with him], which was exceptionally traumatising. . . . I was just thinking [about my body], in the way of it wasn't mine . . . I didn't consent. . . . But I was so numb to it, and I just felt like it was such an overwhelming hit of emotions.*

But it was not just the person she was seeing forcing her to have sex with him after she had been assaulted that underlined the lack of support she had in place at the time. Stella also tried to comfort her in a peculiar way.

> *She said, 'If it makes you feel better, he only ever dates models'.*

Stella's comment reiterated the associations Courtney had made between being sexually assaulted and feeling validated by the male attention.

> *The comment didn't make me feel better about what happened. But it did make me think, 'Oh . . . someone thinks I'm good looking'. . . . That gave me a bit of confidence boost, if I'm to be truthful. But in saying that, I still didn't feel better about what happened and I still didn't feel like that justified anything.*

Despite the comment being unsettling, Stella did support Courtney in going to the police, acknowledging that what happened was not acceptable, nor was it her fault. On the other hand, Betty tried to suggest Courtney was partially responsible. Courtney no longer relied on Betty to escape her homelife as she had more friends. So when Betty made this comment, Courtney ended her friendship with her.

> *Even though her comment was terrible, I think I'm quite desensitised . . . but she still supported me taking action. . . .*
> *[Betty] was like, 'Well, no, you're an idiot . . . it was probably, like, partially your fault . . . you could have led him on.' . . . So, . . . I was just so sick of that crap and sick of that world.*

Moved out of home

Not long after she had a falling out with Betty, Courtney decided to move out of her mother's house to live closer to the city with Stella. She had saved up a substantial amount of money and was able to find work at a patisserie, but this was still a significant loss of financial and emotional support. As a result, Courtney's eating disorder behaviours significantly increased.

> *When I moved out I definitely had a flare up . . . just that overwhelming nature of . . . being pushed out into the rental life. . . . I obviously saved a lot, so I was*

never without. But, I immediately set myself up with a job . . . so I always had like free bread, or like cheaper food.

Courtney's relationships with her immediate family also changed. Her parents were not visiting her often, so she would need to visit them. Her family, who had once been the most amazing part of her life, were now only really seeing her when she put the effort in to drive to their houses.

I was also alone, like with my thoughts. . . . I was very proud as well, I didn't want to ask my parents for any help and dad was in a new relationship . . . mum's not comfortable driving far—so it was like, both of them weren't visiting me. . . . My sister visited me way more than mum and dad, I'd always have to go and visit them . . . so yeah I had a pretty big . . . downfall with the whole eating habit stuff.

Body-image

With Courtney's increased weight-loss behaviours came increased body-image monitoring.

I used to bend to the side and see how many rolls of skin I'd have. But it's like, there was no fat there, that was just my skin. . . . I even used to measure my thighs, used to measure my waist. You know, I used to keep a diary of all my measurements, and I'd do it monthly. . . . I used to be obsessed with scales, but then I didn't trust them.

It was not just her own body that Courtney monitored, it was also the people around her, comparing herself to them constantly.

I used to judge everyone. It wasn't even necessarily someone that was overweight, it was literally any body shape. I just judged it . . . I'm not meaning necessarily even in the sense of, 'Oh, that's disgusting', or, 'That's really hot'. . . . It was like that scrutinising . . . comparing everybody like really obsessively. . . . And then if there was something that I thought looked good, or if they pulled it off, I'd be like, 'Why can't I?'

No matter what, I'd notice their clothing, and I'd look at how it sat on them . . . not necessarily judging, just analysing . . . it wasn't always to do with the actual body.

Friends: Ignorance is bliss

Courtney's eating disorder behaviours were often ignored or normalised by her friends. This confirmed to Courtney that her value was based on her appearance, and that not doing these behaviours would compromise her worthiness.

Stella: "Oh that's just what [Courtney] struggles with"

Living with Stella, Courtney's behaviours became normalised and were not addressed in any way that was conducive of recovery.

It was kind of like, 'Oh that's just what [Courtney] struggles with'. . . . I'd come home, sometimes with a whole cheesecake. I remember once . . . sitting there eating part of this thing, and then just getting a knife out and stabbing it . . . all that was met with was, 'Oh man I didn't get any cheesecake', like from my housemate . . . it was considered normal behaviour for me to be so flippant and emotional.

By normalising or ignoring Courtney's behaviours, Stella was able to engage in her own maladaptive behaviours without judgement from Courtney.

She took abuse more in the sense of, like . . . heavy drinking and she'd always push me to do the same . . . she'd always condone the bad behaviour, and we fed off of each other massively.
She loved messy [Courtney], because generally speaking, I'm a very random person . . . and that was heightened during bad mental health episodes. . . . So, yeah, she saw that as fun [Courtney].

Broader friendship group: "We don't want to hear more, because that means we might have to do something"

Courtney had established many new friendships. However, when it came to her eating disorder, there was very little discussion. While some of them knew, only one really showed Courtney that they cared.

A few of my close friends I told. . . . Only one of them cared in the sense of . . . not wanting me to do it. . . . But other friends . . . they were brought up really religious, and . . . with certain types of religious people . . . they get very kind of like, . . . 'Don't ask . . . don't have to deal with it type thing'. . . . If I said anything that was unsettling or upsetting, it'd be like, 'Right. Shut up . . . we don't want to hear more, because that means we might have to do something'. . . . Like one of them was curious and had asked me questions about it, but it was like not curious in the sense of, 'How can we help [Courtney]?' More literally for her own curiosity.

New relationship, new communities, new behaviours

When Courtney was 22, her eating disorder behaviours had significantly decreased, while binge drinking with Stella was still salient. However, Courtney's new relationship with Adam, her now husband, saw major changes in her relationships and communities.

Learning to love . . . mutually

Since her traumatic sexual assaults and nonconsensual encounter when she was 20, Courtney had not engaged in any sexual relations. She had not experienced sex as being something for her, just as something for a man. So, when she had first had sex with Adam, her experience was non-remarkable. However, over time, she was able to feel safe with him and feel more in control of her body. For the first time, her body was not something that was there purely *for* someone else, it was there for her to intimately enjoy *with* someone else.

> *When we first slept together, I felt nothing like absolutely nothing, and I even remember that, because he was so happy . . . never in my life had I ever associated emotion to sex. It has always just been an act of—pretty much pleasure for a man. I'd never gotten anything personally from it at all—until [Adam].*
>
> *. . . Once I started taking down those walls and not being so numb and I guess seeing it as something for both of us . . . the positive things that come, I guess, out of that.*

Maladaptive new communities

Courtney's new relationship also brought with it new audiences and communities. Unfortunately, Adam's family were obsessed with 'healthy' food and body-image, which meant Courtney was again being exposed to body-image discourse.

> *It was hard . . . they had what I would consider a not good relationship with food coupled with an obsession to not be overweight. So, it wasn't a good thing . . . and they're very fat-shaming people, like, heavily.*

They also often discussed Adam's ex-girlfriend, making Courtney seem inferior in comparison.

> *Even his mum going on about how gorgeous she was . . . but you know, never comment on myself, being the new relationship.*

These comparisons also came from Adam's friendship group who had all gone to high school with Adam and his girlfriend. On one night out, a man who knew Adam's ex-girlfriend made some particularly nasty comments about Courtney's appearance.

> *The belittling like . . . 'You must have a good personality . . . to make up for the looks'. . . . He went on this tangent. But . . . I think because I've received so much over my life, I've always kind of just shut up. Standing up myself, it's not something I'm good at.*

Courtney subsequently began to engage more frequently in her eating disorder behaviours to reclaim some control.

> *I was bulimic and then I had a lull, and then I went downhill again. And yeah, it's honestly about the time that I was having to put up with his lot, once I met [Adam] . . . it really started up again.*

Healthy new communities . . . and hopes for future

Courtney relapsed into her comfortable eating disorder behaviours where she had complete control. However, while Adam had reintroduced some negative communities and discourses into her life, Courtney was also introduced to a new community that had the opposite effect. Adam's closest friends, the people who mattered to him the most, behaved in a way that was so far removed from Courtney's previous communities.

> *I was quite happy with doing [eating disorder behaviours] at the time because it felt like control, because everything else was so messy. . . . It's like I already knew that my lifestyle wasn't healthy, . . . but I think there's a difference between knowing and then experiencing. So then when I was out with [Adam] and his mates . . . they're very like, 'Have a beer and have a laugh', . . . nothing sexualised . . . I think that that helped me kind of shift my thinking.*

Another thought that changed Courtney's thinking around her eating disorder was the new desire to have a baby.

> *And the other thing . . . I know that bulimia can obviously affect fertility. So . . . I don't know why that started festering at the back of my mind like, 'What if I'm ruining my body of having any chances?'*

Relationships and homes . . . out with the old, in with the new

It was not just the addition of Adam's communities that changed for Courtney. Her existing relationship with Stella also became rocky.

> *[Stella] was upset when [Adam] and I first got together, because obviously then I wasn't going out with her and . . . it put more light, I think onto her bad behaviours when I was being . . . you know, good . . . whatever that pertains to.*

Over the course of ten months, Courtney's relationship with Stella became progressively worse and eventually they had a falling out and Courtney decided to move out. However, she did not want to move back in with her parents and so she moved in with Adam despite their relationship being fresh.

> *We moved in together when we were ten months together, . . . and that's because I had that huge fallout with [Stella]. . . . I practically begged [Adam]. I was like, 'I know we're early in the relationship, but I can't move back home, I'm not ready'.*

Recovery

Courtney's behaviours got progressively better over the years, and she began to identify as recovered. She and Adam moved farther away from his family to be closer to her family, meaning she had more support in place. However, that came with a level of blame directed at Courtney from Adam's family.

> *This is what it used to be . . . 'She's taken him away to the coast to be near her family'. . . . But it was actually [Adam], who was like, 'Nah we're moving back down near your family'. . . . Even though his parents knew that, they still blamed me for his apparent brainwashing.*

Becoming a mother

Pregnancy

It was at the age of 25, when Courtney found out she was pregnant that her behaviours completely stopped.

> *I started putting weight on again, and that was actually really hard because I was fully recovered, obviously, by that stage. . . . So I had a struggle there. But then when I started going downhill—I didn't start my bulimia again—but when I started having those thoughts again, you know, pretty much, [Adam] and I started looking for a house and that was just like distraction, and then it was like, 'Oh crap you're pregnant, okay'. It was a bit of a rollercoaster, no time to do it again. . . .*
>
> *I probably stopped when I found out I was pregnant . . . a lot of my mental health issues were . . . I feel forced to stop because of getting pregnant and becoming a mum and it was like . . . you don't think of yourself anymore.*

Traumatic birth

When Courtney gave birth, she had a complete loss of control. She was in pain, and naked when she did not want to be.

> *I was naked, and I did not want to be naked . . . I put that under that whole non-consensual—because . . . in the end, you really do lose a lot of control because you're just in too much pain . . . there I am, naked as fuck, and I have this pathetic towel over me, but I was too agitated by it touching me but it's like, I just felt so exposed, and all I wanted was at least my bra, just to feel some comfort.*

Courtney was also not taken seriously when she told the medical team that her baby was stuck until she finally managed to be alone with Adam. So, while she was the one giving birth, her pain was not taken seriously until it was voiced by her partner.

> *My only time alone with [Adam] . . . I was just like, 'You need to get aggressive'. . . . then finally a couple of doctors came in . . . and that's when they gave each other the look and it was just like [Adam] had to sign a waiver . . . that is a pain that I will forever have.*

The wrong type of attention

After her traumatic labour, Courtney was physically unwell and as a result, she lost weight. Despite this being as a result of physical trauma and was making caring for her newborn baby difficult, Adam's family praised her for the weight-loss.

> *I got really sick, I lost something like 1.6 litres of blood. . . . I'm naturally a size 10 to 12 . . . and I went down to a size 6 to 8. . . . I remember the dad saying to me, 'Oh you look really good though'.*
>
> *I once heard behind my back, as well, [Adam's father] was saying to [Adam] . . . '[Courtney] is not one of those lazy mums who just packs on the weight', . . . and there I am like, wishing I could put weight on . . . that's just a disgusting thing to say.*

Despite these comments, Courtney, for the first time in her life, was able to allow her "logical" side to win against her "eating disorder" side.

> *I felt really good about the weight-loss, honestly. But I didn't feel well . . . my logical side and my . . . eating disorder side, were kind of having a big battle. . . .*
>
> *. . . Don't get me wrong, I had a lot of trouble, but like the logical side had never won before . . . it never had a strong enough voice, and it truly was once [my daughter] came along . . . I just kept thinking, 'I need to eat'.*

Adam's parents continued to interject, making Courtney's body seem repulsive when she breastfed her baby.

> *I was belittled, very, very heavily for breastfeeding . . . going on about me having sour tit milk.*

Now a mother . . . Where is the father?

Adam, on the other hand, was not involved enough. Courtney desperately wanted him to help with the parenting, but he did not offer that support.

> *If something is happening to me, he kind of freaks out and shuts down . . . he'll have his own freakouts . . . particularly after [our first-born] . . . I desperately needed help, but I never got the help. . . . He got a semi-diagnosis of postnatal depression. . . . But I really do feel like he used it as a tool of power to pretty much justify his lack of involvement at the beginning.*

This was difficult for Courtney as it was very similar behaviour to her father being absent when she was a child and how that changed her family unit monumentally. They did, however, go on to get married and have a second baby. Fortunately, Adam was much more helpful with their second child.

Navigating life now

Courtney identifies as being recovered from her eating disorder; however, there are still remnants in her daily life.

Tactile cues for body-image thinking

While she often does not think very actively about her body-image, there are cues that spark these thoughts.

> *If I'm aware of where I'm sitting, or . . . looking in my peripheral down below, it's like, I could feel my arms on my legs. I can feel them touching. I don't like how they touch my legs . . . like I feel like that area where I've put on weight like touching an area that it shouldn't be touching and like I get really ultra, I guess hyper aware of . . . what I'm not satisfied with . . . it gets worse if I'm in a bad headspace. . . .*
>
> *I don't like things brushing against me. . . . For example, a baggy shirt, I don't like it twisting on me, I don't like if there is a breeze, I don't like that—I've got no problem if it were just the breeze on its own, say on my skin, but I don't like it passing, and like, moving my clothing on me . . . I don't like the awareness of my body parts. . . .*
>
> *It still pops into my head every day . . . say I'm putting pants on . . . I will watch my legs, and like I will look at myself sitting and—well pretty much just judge if they look different than normal. Like have they changed? . . . It's always a case of making sure they're the same as the day before.*

Fear has a time and a place

"Looking the part" is a behaviour that Courtney learnt from her extended family on her father's side. While she socially distanced from them when she was younger, she still learnt that how you present yourself is an important social behaviour.

> *I have a fear of looking like shit, while going to the shops . . . out of fear that someone will recognise me. And, yeah, not think that I look good. . . . I don't like the thought of anyone from my past, thinking that I'm not doing well. But because I won't let them in on my life . . . the only way that I see that can be translated is through physical appearance.*

While Courtney's body-image concerns remain prevalent, she censors what she says in front of her children as she does not want them to know that she has these thoughts.

> *I desperately try not to show the kids. . . . I'm pretty much just lying through my teeth to them, to make sure that they don't see how I really am.*

Courtney's experience with her mother's poor mental health has been a major driver in her recovery. While she does not blame her mother for her experience, she is also aware that when mental disorders take over parents' behaviours, it can be difficult for the children to understand.

> *It's all well and good to have a crappy day, or to feel stressed, as long as . . . if you do anything stupid, you make sure the kids know it's not their fault. . . . But then on the other side it's like if I were a bulimic, how the hell do you . . . hide that from your kids? . . . It's not possible, it comes out. . . . I'm not trying to be like some wonder woman that doesn't have her faults, it's more the extent of the fault.*

What we can learn from Courtney

Courtney's eating disorder followed a series of major changes in her once perfect homelife. Seeking stability in another home meant conforming to their values in the form of weight-loss behaviours and allowing herself to be sexualised by the men around her. These behaviours were often a way for her to assert control when her life felt very 'out of control'.

However, pregnancy and motherhood were pivotal in her recovery. She had seen her mother go from being the perfect role model to struggling to leave the house. Courtney's recovery is fuelled by a desire to remain well for her children's well-being.

13 Katrina's story

What goes on behind closed doors

Katrina was shocked when she was diagnosed at the age of 26 and did not initially accept the diagnosis of anorexia nervosa and avoidant and restrictive food intake disorder. With therapists, Katrina unpacked that avoiding food and staying small made her feel safe—it was a trauma response. Katrina had many traumatic experiences across her life including car accidents, sexual assaults and the death of a partner, but the most prominent trauma in her story was "emotionally neglectful" parents. Katrina understood these traumatic events to have made long-term changes to her nervous system. But from a contextual perspective, the broader conditions of these events continued to be shaping forces over time.

Early childhood

"My first introduction to feeding wasn't super fab"

Baby Katrina suffered feeding difficulties with her mother, including an allergy to her milk formula, but once these issues were resolved, Katrina continued to refuse and avoid food. When her parents consulted doctors, they were told Katrina was just a fussy eater, and advised to keep feeding her without bringing too much attention to it.

> From a very young age, I used to feed the dog . . . and throwing food away all the way through school because I just had this real inability to eat it, it was a real block.

"She had to deal or else, then she feels like she'd let their partnership down"

Katrina's parents had not planned to have children, and her mother had little support with caregiving due to geographical and social isolation. Her parents lived on a family-run farm, where her paternal grandparents were their closest neighbours at a half-hour drive. After Katrina's birth, her mother had thoughts of not being a mother and thoughts of suicide.

DOI: 10.4324/9781003453918-15

That era where it was like, 'Oh, well, it's women's business' having a baby. . . .
[Dad] grew up in quite a traditional household so he went back to work straight up.
   She also felt a bit of pressure I think because my dad didn't really want children
at all. . . . Their group of friends, she was like, 'I was eight years behind them hav-
ing children' . . . didn't really know if she wanted one, but then did, and so wasn't
a naturally very maternal person anyway, and then had me, and it really threw her.
   Early '90s, not a lot was known about or spoken about with postnatal depression,
particularly in country towns . . . mental health was really taboo.

"That was really the beginning of the end for their marriage"

When Katrina was 3, her father had a car accident resulting in significant physical injuries, including injuries to the brain. After physical rehabilitation, tasks
that were once easy remained difficult, and he acted short with a lot of people.

His personality changed quite significantly from being quite a happy-go-lucky person
to a very kind of hard, straight down the line, emotionally cold person. My mum
suffered a lot. . . . Mum says that she married one person and 10 years later she had
another person who she was living with.

"I lived there for 10 years of my life, and it just never felt like home"

When she was 9, Katrina's family relocated to a distant rural town far from
friends and relatives. They relocated so her father could continue his career in
local politics, but on weekends he travelled back to the farm. In the new town,
Katrina's mother found work in a local business, but she struggled to establish
close friendships.

My grandparents who were getting on elderly, and we ran a farm, and so there was
like a lot of responsibility to stay . . . so dad was still driving back and I think my
mum and dad's marriage started to kind of, that's when for me, I really recognised
that it deteriorated.
   It was really hard on my mum because mum didn't instantly kind of find connec-
tion to community either . . . people would really want to be her friend because of my
dad's job. . . . The minute they couldn't influence my dad through her, they kind of
dropped her. . . . People believe that the CEO make the decisions around like having
a road upgraded, having this added, or funds going to this art show.

School years

"It was interesting because I would never have defied my parents on anything else like that. No way"

Katrina avoided her eating being spoken about in the community, but in the
privacy at home, she openly fought with her parents about eating. She rebuffed

their efforts to influence her eating through rewards, punishments, criticism, guilt and lessons in cooking. Katrina would say that cooking was boring, plus it was too hard because she had to wash her hands anytime she touched food and did not like ingredients to mix. At age 12, Katrina identified as vegetarian and frequently vocalised her ethical reasons for avoiding meat.

> *I didn't want people to talk about my food a lot . . . friends' houses and their parents just, 'You should eat more, you need more, you're so tiny'. And I'd be [thinking] like, 'No, I don't want to, don't tell me what I need to do' . . . but I had to walk that line of wanting to be good and polite and kind.*
>
> *Dinner times were nightmares . . . because I didn't want to eat, they would fight with one another . . . mum would tell me that I was hurt-like, 'I put in so much effort for dinner and you're not appreciating it', but then she'd also try and protect me from dad cause dad would come down so hard on me. I would end up crying. I'd have to stay at the table until I had eaten everything . . . 6 until 18, that was pretty much nearly every dinner.*

Although her parents criticised larger bodies, Katrina did not think much about her body, especially critical thoughts about her weight or appearance. If anything, she had concerns about not appearing womanly enough.

> *My parents are quite fat phobic in the way that they talk about people, particularly my father, he's a very critical person. . . . I wasn't consciously trying to shrink my body . . . I'd always been the tall skinny girl and I just was okay with that.*
>
> *My friends were these women, and I still felt like I was a child. I remember having a lot of concerns around that and wanting to put on clothes that my friends were wearing.*

"It was very quiet and so much seething underneath, and yes so much going on unsaid"

Katrina's homelife was uncomfortably quiet due to the unaddressed conflict between her parents, and little affection shared between family members. Katrina's maternal relatives were nurturing, but they lived far away. Being an only child, Katrina spent much time alone in her room reading or writing in her journal.

> *My parents sometimes with each other would try and be really polite to each other so I wouldn't see it, but I did, I was like, 'I know exactly what's going on here'. . . . I knew my parents didn't love each other, from a very young age. . . . I have it written in a journal when I'm 11 saying, 'I don't think my parents love each other, I think they're gonna break up'.*
>
> *Weren't a very huggy family, mum was kind of huggy, my dad wasn't at all. I remember being little and I'd say to him like, 'I love you' and he'd be like, 'Okay'. . . . That was pretty standard for me . . . our family's not very warm. . . .*

There wasn't a lot of other expression . . . the normal flat like, 'How was school today?', 'Yeah, it was fine', 'Okay'.

My auntie, she's someone who I would like cuddle a lot . . . she's very, very warm and loving. . . . I would always feel safe when I—I still do, I still feel really safe when I'm with her and same with my grandma. But it's interesting, I just don't have that relationship with my mum.

"I just didn't ever trust my parents to react the way that I wanted them to"

Katrina's parents often responded to her expressions of distress with frustration, annoyance, criticism or blame. At age 12, Katrina was in a collision while being driven home by her baby-sitter. She sustained injuries and witnessed horrific scenes, but her parents did not seek any medical or therapeutic support and Katrina returned to school as soon as possible. As Katrina got older and more aware of how her parents minimised her distress, she fantasised about self-harm that might evoke real concern from them.

I had every sort of survival need met obviously, plus more, I never really went without things . . . a lot of care but just if I had really strong emotions I was told, 'Calm down, you're being silly' just like, 'You're okay, you're making this a big thing out of nothing' and so, my emotions were wrong and inconvenient. . . . 'You're being dramatic' was a big thing like, 'You're very dramatic', and we were very, as a family very much like, you just get on with things.

The minute they could just sweep it under the rug and like, 'Back to school, you're fine' kind of thing. They thought that was the way of dealing with it . . . when I was 15 . . . I couldn't walk properly and then I'd have to go to the physio. . . . When my mum wasn't in the room the physio said to me, 'Oh, have you had any work on this done prior cause you had a really significant accident?' . . . and I was like, 'No, this is the first time because I can't walk'. And I remember her shaking her head.

I was about 16 or 17 and I was driving, and I used to just think about, 'it would really show them if I just ran off the road', stuff like that.

"Dad found it really easy to be 'the CEO' but who he was, was a different story"

By the time Katrina was age 13, her family had settled further into the new town following the passing of her grandparents and the sale of the farm. Katrina's father established himself as a prominent person in the new community through his leadership positions, and he expected his wife and daughter to play their role in the perfect family.

If I look back on both of my parents, they weren't really very authentic . . . the way they are when they're around other people, they're not who they are. It's always with who is watching, who was judging.

That kind of like small town prestige thing as well, we'd go to these bloody events that was so boring and I would just dress up and mum would dress up. . . . You'd hear them talk about us, like think that we just this amazing family who lives in the house with, the big house on the hill with all things, and I just, now it just makes me go, 'Wow like it's so funny isn't it, that we just don't know what goes on behind closed doors'.

There's always hierarchies and there's a lot of politics, and I think my parents really just, I think they really did want the best for me, and they thought the best for me was maintaining this profile.

"I had such strong conditioning that it reduced my autonomy"

From a young age, Katrina was praised by her parents for being good, which meant being polite, well-behaved and generally not causing a fuss. In secondary school, being good also meant achieving academically and avoiding parties.

To look at me, you wouldn't have said, 'Oh, like she's so under the thumb by her parents', I wasn't that. But my conditioning around having to be good and having to perform and to be a perfectionist and do really well, meant that I was kind of a bit of their puppet. . . . In terms of expectations, I just, I would just always rise to meet it . . . I guess that was how I got attention . . . unless I was being praised, I didn't know where I stood.

I don't think I knew any different when I was little, I thought that everyone's parents held them up to the same expectations as mine. . . . I remember my dad just being like, 'Why did you get a C?' . . . and I'm like, 'You know I don't like sport' and he was like, 'Yeah but you should still do well enough to get an A, this like ruined your report'.

When we'd be at family things, or even their friends when they'd have like dinners, they'd be like, '[Katrina] tell what you were just talking to me about blah blah blah' because it would have been a bit of a, I don't know, 'my daughter knows things' or whatever.

"It was such a bitchy place . . . even from adults, everyone knew everyone's business"

Katrina experienced the town to be full of gossip, politics, superficial friendships and a homogenous culture with little room for difference.

I remember my friend's parents, her father cheated on her mother, and it was public knowledge, and people were speaking about it in the grocery shops and the bakery, and it was the butchers, people just spoke about people's stuff so regularly.

There was a girl . . . she was about five years older than me, but she had anorexia in our town, and that's all she was known as, was 'the girl with anorexia'. . . . It was this really big taboo subject . . . she just was on her own all the time, was very socially isolated.

"I spent so much of my time particularly in school like watching my back"

Katrina's family status and good girl performance made her a target for bullying, and she had little escape with only 20 people in her cohort. Katrina had one close friend who moved away as she entered secondary school, and others distanced themselves to avoid being bullied by association. In a town that revolved around sports and parties, Katrina had little ways of influencing her peers, because she did not excel at sports and her father did not allow her to attend parties.

> *I was always called a snob, in the town everyone knew me as the snob. . . . People thought I was a snob because my parents had money. . . . I bought a car when I was 17 and people just made fun of me for that, and they egged my car. . . . I was bullied significantly for being what did they say, 'too perfect'.*
>
> *I had these expectations from my parents to be a certain person and I thought I was doing that right, but then I had peers then telling me because I was trying to do that then I was—yeah I was in this kind of vice, it was a really hard place to be in.*

"I really didn't have a sense of self . . . I had a lot of people telling me who I was"

Katrina gained influence with peers when she made relationships outside of her cohort. She befriended older students at school through dance and met a boyfriend who was a year older from a different school. But more relationships also introduced more expectations, and some conflicted with one another. Towards the end of school, Katrina started to break school rules, dress differently, join parties and lie to her parents.

> *They [parents] always let me go if I was with my boyfriend . . . they say that I can look after myself really well, and then say on the other hand, 'Oh you need a man to look after to you'.*
>
> *I would just go and just do all the naughty things, all the things I wasn't allowed to do, and then try and come back and regain and save face . . . put my persona back together again.*
>
> *I used to get a lot of, 'You're better than this' or 'You're not like the other kids' or 'You're smarter than this' . . . 'Remember who you are, remember what family you come from'. . . . The language that was used a lot was like, 'Oh, but that's not you, you're not like that, this is what you're like'.*
>
> *I felt as if he [boyfriend] wanted someone who was a perfect princess . . . looking back, I just think that was more so, more and more, his parents' expectations . . . they went to church a lot and my family didn't do that all. . . . I think he used to get kind of embarrassed or a bit like 'just like put a lid on it' or something.*

"I had no one in my corner at that stage"

In her graduating year, Katrina's boyfriend ended the relationship because he was struggling to transition into university. Katrina continued to go out to parties and met someone new, who assaulted her.

> He broke up with me, that's when I spiralled a bit . . . drinking a lot and kind of sleeping around. . . . I started to see a guy . . . he ended up being quite predatory and he sexually assaulted me. And I didn't tell anyone because he told me it was my fault and I believed him.
>
> I would still see him at the football club . . . local pub with my friends and he'd be there. . . . I cut this guy out, but I had to see him and I also, I just saw the way the town idolised him. He was this a-grade footballer and so everyone is just like 'he's such a good guy, such an amazing person' . . . they were like, 'Oh yeah, but he does that and he's still a really cool dude and he's still great'.
>
> I started acting out, kind of around the time that I was seeing him, and then after that, I guess I say acting out I was, I don't know, traumatised or whatever.
>
> They [parents] could see that the town probably wasn't super fantastic for me. Dad still wanted me to come back and play for the netball club and he still wanted me to be a big part of the town. But the minute I moved out, I became quite vocal about, I used to say, 'I hate this town, I hate it so much, it's fucked up, people here shit'.

Graduation and working

"It was like a socially acceptable eating disorder. Basically no one could pick at me because of like 'oh no, she's a vegan'"

Leaving home, Katrina had strong ideas about 'good' and 'bad' foods. She participated in wellness culture and yoga, which she shared with some friends. Her eating was restricted by rules around ethics, health, wellness and perceived food intolerances. If Katrina broke her eating rules, then she compensated with restriction and cleansing rituals using special health products. Despite being undernourished, Katrina was spending hundreds of dollars at health food stores.

> If I had all these foods that I couldn't eat, then when we went out for dinner . . . I could just have the salad and people would be like, 'Oh yeah, but she can't eat gluten, so the salad'.

"Why would I even think that I had an issue? Because the social standards, I was winning"

While some people would occasionally question Katrina's eating or body size, for the most part, she received compliments and economic opportunities for her practices.

*I was living in a body that people were like, 'Oh that's great, look at you, oh gosh
I wish I looked like you, I wish I was thin and tall like you' and how even I was a
model and I was getting paid to look that way, so why would I change?*

"My parents who were these two super solid people just came crumbling down in that time, so I felt like I had no sort of security"

After graduation, Katrina accepted a journalism cadetship in a neighbouring
town and moved into her parents' second property. Katrina enjoyed living alone,
but her parents separated not long after and her mother joined her. The divorce
did not improve her relationship with her parents, and their expectations of her
did not change. Katrina avoided her parents by spending time with her new
partner and his friends.

*When I moved out . . . I think mum was more upset because then she had to really
face if she wanted to stay with my father . . . they always say they did it [stayed
together] for me, but I think that was pretty crap.*

*My parents' divorce really affected my eating . . . it got worse absolutely,
because . . . my mum moved in with me . . . she would see this guy this weekend
and this guy this weekend, and I was like 'who the hell's my mum?'*

*When they broke up, I struggled a lot because it was, 'Oh, you're so adult about
this, you're doing so well about this', but I was like well I didn't really get a chance
to be anything else, you've just told me that I'm fine, you've just told me that I'm
adult, about it . . . after the divorce, there was just a bit of bad blood. I was just a
little bit over them, and so I was quite avoidant.*

*It was great because he [partner] lived in the hills and so I would travel up there
and meeting a whole new group of people who I thought were awesome, and so it
just gave me a really good out. . . . It was a very different life because it wasn't about
saving face, it was just kind of about living, and living well and camping. . . . I
started to meet people who I really vibed with, I was like, 'Oh, this is friendship'.*

"I got into a very adult life before, way before, I needed to be there"

Katrina took a short break from journalism to study naturopathy and moved to
the city with her partner. She also had an opportunity to go overseas for modelling, but her partner did not approve. Katrina's partner wanted to move back to
the hills, so they bought a house together, and Katrina dropped out of naturopathy to return to journalism. Their relationship began to deteriorate, but neither
of them initiated a breakup.

*I think he was looking for someone who was like wife material. . . . I really got locked
into a very adult life at 22, like home, dog, him, full-time job as a journo, building
another house . . . we were breaking up for two years, two years out of six we were
breaking up, but we didn't, neither of us wanted to kind of admit it and so that was
really stressful.*

"What we learn from our parents, I guess we apply for ourselves"

After her partner blocked new work opportunities, journalism kept her trapped within the expectations of everyone else, with little time for spontaneity. The news cycle was demanding, she worked hard to compete with others with more experience or education, and her editor did not approve the "social justice" stories that she preferred.

> *I spent a bit of time in my late-teens, early-20s trying to kind of remove the good girl label, but I definitely feel like I moved back into it pretty quick. . . . I was like, 'I'm good, I'm good at life, look at how good I am, I'm disciplined, I'm not partying heaps with my friends, I'm focusing a lot of my studies, look how disciplined I am, and I'm eating, eating perfectly, or as perfectly as I could, look at how good I am'.*
>
> *I'd created this life where everything was so predictable and I was like, 'How did I get here? Because everyone else was telling me here is where I'm meant to be, and I'm so unhappy'. . . . I didn't feel lit up at all. I was just going through the motions of life.*

"I decided to quit my job to become a yogi which caused a lot of ripples and a lot of drama"

Katrina travelled overseas with friends to train in yoga teaching, which provided distance to separate from her partner. She moved in with her mother until the separation was finalised, then into a share house with her friends. Katrina worked in a yoga studio which she supplemented with hospitality work and enrolled in an online counselling course.

> *I really had really fashioned myself as a very dependable person in a lot of people's lives, so for me to leave and pack up and go was quite big. . . . My parents they treated it, particularly my dad, treated that as a phase, 'Oh she's just going through a phase, oh she will go back to journalism soon'. . . . I just wanted to break free so much of who I felt that they believed I was, and I went I got tattoos and then did all of those kinds of things.*

"I really lost the good girl because I'm like 'well she's long gone', like I just didn't feel like that anymore"

Katrina's new life came to a halt when the man she was seeing died from an overdose. To grieve, she took leave from work and moved in with her mother, but being close with her parents was not helpful. Katrina's friends supported her in her grief, but being in the city was too much of a reminder of her loss.

> *My parents didn't particularly handle his loss very well. My mum swooped in and wanted to suddenly play mother and keep me safe and it was really like 'urgh' I didn't want her to do that. . . . Dad was just like, 'Let's not talk about it and let's make you happy by taking you on wine tours'.*

People would see me in the streets and be like, 'I'm so sorry' and just coming up and I just didn't want to be that girl whose boyfriend had died . . . everywhere I looked was places that we had gone to and places that we had existed within together. . . . It was also for me a fear I failed, like okay I was studying addictions and I hadn't got him the help.

My family saw me as someone who had so much potential but who failed to reach it. . . . My parents were always like, 'Oh, what's gone wrong now' kind of thing . . . in the last five years I had lost the person I thought I would marry and then I met someone new and I'd lost him physically, and then I had a few assaults . . . and things not going right. . . . There was a lot of instability. . . . I lost a lot of ideas about what I, who I thought I was.

"It was the straw that broke the camel's back"

Katrina rebuilt her life quickly, which introduced a lot of change. On an inter-state trip with her friends, she met someone new, and she relocated to join him. She found work in a yoga studio, continued to study counselling online and eventually moved in with her partner who worked away. Back home, Katrina knew the different sub-cultures and where her group fit, but in her new city she observed a homogenous ideal that she did not align with.

I've enjoyed the break and the space to be whoever I wanted to be without people having a backstory of who I was . . . when I moved up here, it was like I had room to breathe, and that's when everything came crashing down.

I was kind of alone for a bit, and I was out of my normal environment, and that felt scary for me. That's when I started to really not eat or micromanage and then I realised that okay I didn't really look like the people out here and I wasn't toned so I've got to do a lot of Pilates and I've got to do a lot of yoga . . . up here it really is quite like a one standard of beauty . . . well-maintained people, when I say that like going to the gym every single day. . . . That active lifestyle comes from the weather, it's always warm . . . so people have their bodies out on show.

Diagnosis and recovery

"I was thinking, 'Oh, shit, something's wrong, something's actually wrong'"

Katrina lost strength and energy and found it difficult to complete daily tasks. She saw multiple doctors to investigate her symptoms, until a young female doctor asked her questions about eating and referred her to a specialist clinic. Katrina was diagnosed with *anorexia nervosa* and retrospectively with avoidant and restrictive food intake disorder, and offered outpatient treatment by a psychologist and a nutritionist. Katrina was not convinced that she had an eating disorder, but she wanted the medical and therapeutic support. Katrina's treatment team explained that her resistance to their diagnosis and treatment was her 'disordered self'.

I was just like, 'No, this is not, it's not me at all, but I'll just go and humour them for one session'. . . . I was still very caught up in in what health was from very much a wellness state and so when she was saying to me, 'You've just got to eat really simple carbs because your body's not digesting complex carbs'. I was like 'Gross, you're wrong, you don't understand health'. . . . I didn't believe that I was sick enough because we had this idea that anorexia looks like complete emancipation . . . I ended up having heart issues . . . got a heart monitor and I've had an ECG and I've had some ultrasounds on my heart and that started to kind of wake me up.

I really liked the psychological support and then I didn't because she started really pushing my buttons. . . . We talked a lot about the healthy self and the disordered self. . . . I could just feel this expression within me, and it was so rigid and angry . . . when I would be talking to the psych and they'd be telling me what they want me to do and I would just be like, 'Fuck off, you're trying to take something'. It was weird, it's like they're trying to take something from me even though I hadn't even acknowledged that I had this thing . . . an incredible amount of resistance, 'You can't tell me what to do, don't tell me what to do'.

"Recovery made me more aware of my body-image than I felt prior to being diagnosed"

When Katrina followed the nutritionist's advice and put on weight, she had new thoughts about her body, that it was not okay to be getting bigger. Katrina hated to think of herself as a shallow person, but she could not deny that she associated fatness with being less-than or being weak.

I just didn't even pick up that I had this body, I didn't think about it in those ways . . . when I did start putting weight on a lot of the behaviours like body checking and weighing myself and that really started when I started recovery. . . . Once that had really made itself known, I went, 'Okay, there's an issue here' and then I started to kind of come around, but it took me about a year to fully recognise that I was, that I had an eating disorder.

"I wasn't 'well', then I went into 'disorder', then I 'came out', like my whole life was disordered"

While a fear of fatness did arise during treatment, Katrina did not relate to the stories of others with anorexia nervosa. Katrina explored her life history with her family and discussed this with her treatment team, who told her she had "the perfect storm" for an eating disorder: early feeding difficulties and choking incidents, emotionally distant parents, trauma, perfectionism and societal pressures.

The origins of my disorder are based in trauma, they're not based in wanting to look a certain way. But the culture that we live in definitely, I believe, perpetuated my disorder.

Part of my recovery was very much like writing letters to the ED and thanking it for what it had done . . . it was the coping mechanism, the only one that I could work with at such a young age.

That kind of habit of minimisation is something that I've taken into my own life and when I've had some really big things happen to me, I really minimise the things that happened and made it all kind of my fault and then I've spent the last three, four years of my life unpacking all of that.

I'm reading a book . . . it's about, where did dieting come from and where this want for women to be so thin and so obedient and contained has come from, and so that's fired me up a bit. . . . In the book, it talks a lot about like a good girl archetype and I definitely saw that. . . . I've unpacked with psychs, being good made me feel safe, it was a safety mechanism just as much as being small.

"They never just allowed me to be fucked up essentially . . . I was really only accountable to myself"

People in Katrina's life responded to her eating disorder in varied ways. Some misunderstood her eating to be an easily changed choice or efforts to be more beautiful. Her yogi friends who were more spiritual than scientific, did not validate her trauma narrative. Her parents did help construct her trauma narrative through conversations, but they minimised the seriousness of her condition and offered little support.

Most of my friends are yogis, right, and people with these kinds of spiritual ideations and that say like, 'Oh, don't make that your story, don't take that on'.

[Parter] he's had a real crash course into eating disorder and understanding them. It's been really fantastic. He has struggled a little bit with understanding it completely. . . . I'm pretty lucky because he is someone who works in rehabilitation, mental health rehabilitation setting . . . and we both kind of had similar traumatic incidences in our lives.

My parents have no concept around mental health. . . . I tried to try to educate them, and they did a bit of education, but not a lot.

I found myself ringing them [parents] and saying like, 'I'm not okay. I'm really fucked up essentially, I'm really fucked up', and they would say to me 'but you are okay, and you can get through anything, and you know that'. And I would really sometimes go over like, 'I want to die'. I'd say these things to them because I was kind of wanting them to go, 'Oh my god, you know, you're not okay'. But they never . . . my parents go to me 'Oh, you're just so capable'. . . . They always say that to me and part of me is like, 'Yeah, well, I've had to be, I've had to be capable'.

"I was starting to work as a counsellor and I was like, well I need to be okay if I'm working with people, right?"

Once Katrina persisted with her eating plan until it was no longer as painful or scary, she avoided losing her progress and recovery was sustained. Her treatment team encouraged her to live the recovery story that she could not find herself, and support others going through something similar, so being well enough to work with eating disorder clients was a recovery goal. Katrina's adherence to her eating plan moved her towards credibility as a counsellor and an adult.

> *Something clicked in my head, and it was no longer as hard, and I just wanted to get well, and I wanted to eat, and then from that point to recovery, or to being really fully recovered was quite quick.*
>
> *A real drive was I wanted to work, I wanted to do my work, I love my work, I love being a counsellor. I feel it adds so much meaning and purpose to my life. . . . I find it a lot easier to sit behind my, I guess my labels of who I am: 'counsellor and somatic therapist and yoga teacher'. . . . That's my dad all over again.*
>
> *A lot of shame like 'gosh, I'm 26' and I was at a, you know, a clinic where there was a lot of, you know, 16-year-olds and 18-year-olds and I was here as someone who had lived an adult life, and I was so ashamed that's where I was . . . I was living a half-life, that's what got me through . . . I'm not actually doing life really properly. I'm feeling half of it and I just thought there could be something better, and I wanted to know what that was.*

"My life will probably be to some degree watching this and being aware of it, but . . . the power it has over me no longer exists"

Recovery for Katrina was eating regular meals and snacks across a day, having no dietary restrictions, and accepting weight-gain. She still did not like touching food or mixing ingredients, and still had thoughts of restriction and avoidance, but this did not stop her from eating.

> *My body's still gaining weight slowly so that shows me, and I eat adequately and regularly and a variety, so I'm, as long as my weight's kind of increasing, that's telling me that my body needs it.*
>
> *Full recovery where I no longer have thoughts of avoidance—I don't avoid—but I just don't think that's a reality for me at this point in my life.*
>
> *The disorder was never at the forefront of my mind. . . . I've had a lot of girls counting calories and going through what they've eaten each day at night, and I didn't often do that. It wasn't a super conscious decision, I don't think I had ever consciously gone, 'Oh, well, that felt good, so I'm going to go in and restrict', but because of that I do have to be extra vigilant.*

"I was like, 'wow, she's ballsy' and I'm not—I wasn't playing the good girl"

Katrina's bold behaviour during recovery was attributed to her disordered self, but Katrina did not want to let go of that assertiveness.

> *As I got more and more recovered and I started to see these sides of myself . . . these really honest parts of who I was . . . and I started to really like that person . . . when*

I first saw my psychs I was so sweet and gentle and just whatever they said, I would just be like, 'Okay, yep, cool', and then six months in I was like, 'Fuck off, I'm not doing that'. . . . That was obviously the disorder talking but then once I moved past that, I found this really assertive place where I was like, 'I don't want to be disordered anymore, but this is how I'm going to help myself'.

When Katrina spent time with her friends who ate for wellness, Katrina learnt to assert her new practices around food, bodies and exercise. Katrina challenged the talk of others who criticised larger bodies and she offered alternative ideas such as "health at every size" even if it was not accepted by her audience. Katrina continued to practice and teach yoga with the message that yoga was designed to connect with bodies and not shrink them, and she withdrew from studios that did not align with this message.

Kind of calling that out in people around me . . . they go, 'She shouldn't be wearing a bikini' and I'm like, 'I think she looks fabulous', I kind of counteract that.

I have friends who are vegans and I'm not ashamed to say, 'Look, I'm not anymore like I'm not' and . . . I used to go like 'I'm not anymore because I can't be because I'm recovering' and now I don't feel I even need to validate it with that, I'm just like, 'I just I'm not', that's the end.

"I think they're getting better, but I think maybe that's because my relationship to them have has changed significantly"

The priorities and expectations of Katrina's parents changed as they aged and remarried. Her mother remarried a man who Katrina did not approve of and so they only met without him. Her father remarried a woman with children, retired and recovered his pre-accident personality.

As dad gets older, he mellows out a lot. And I'm starting to see all these expectations he's had for himself too just drop away. . . . He always had really, really big expectations for me, he doesn't now, like he's very different now.

He's really done a big flip backflip . . . really doting on my step siblings' kids, and it's really beautiful to see, but it's hard because it's like that's what I missed out on.

Both parents tried to show Katrina more affection, but Katrina was used to being without their emotional connection. One thing that her parents had always provided was material support, and when they failed to offer financial assistance during Katrina's treatment, this changed her priorities with them.

I've had to process a lot of grief and anger towards them that my life savings, my work as an adult, while I was trying to study to be a counsellor, I was going through some really serious therapy and paying for it, I funded my therapy myself. . . . They have one child that they could have helped out, and they chose not to.

They don't hold much for me anymore, like any power over me, or their opinions don't matter really . . . there's a reason I live here. I love my parents and I have contact with them weekly, each individually, but I just need it, I just need to be here. That's how I live well, is to have distance like this, and to just be able to do completely my own thing.

Part 3

What was learned about unusual eating behaviours put in context?

14 Summary 1

The diversity of life pathways

The nine case studies are rich and long, despite being shorter than the original conversations. In this chapter we wish to move halfway between the long case studies (Chapter 5 to 13) and the brief summary (Chapter 15). Before going over some of the major themes that can be found in the case studies, two provisos need to be kept in mind:

- These themes do not necessarily apply to all the women's contexts.
- These themes do not 'explain' the eating disorders.

We have left the case studies large to help prevent misinterpreting the themes in our summaries as generalisations. While there is a summary pattern to what is happening when eating disorders are shaped (Chapter 15), the nine women's actual lives were a complex mixture of many life contexts. The point being made is that talking about social factors is not as important as exploring how these factors unfolded within their unique contexts, because contextual changes were different for all the women.

The early shaping of eating and body behaviours

The early life stories showed a diversity of behaviours around bodies and eating that *preceded* the beginning of the eating disorder as identified by the women. Table 14.1 shows some of these early behaviours written as short summaries using the women's own words.

Many of these early behaviours related to body size, including monitoring, comparison, critical talk and predicting the words of others. Most of these behaviours had already been *modelled within their groups* like family, school or sports groups, and *caregivers* were prominent in the women's stories as people they observed to talk about their bodies, diet and exercise to lose weight.

Only Katrina restricted food in childhood, and she did this through avoidance and refusal, which was one of the only behaviours available to her at a young age. As she got older and became more verbal, the reasons (discourses) for avoiding eating increased. Societal discourses continued to shape and change the women's eating disorder behaviour over time.

DOI: 10.4324/9781003453918-17

Table 14.1 Early eating and body behaviours prior to the eating disorder.

Adora	Gabby	Diane
• Women are scrutinised for being fat. • "Always look at my bum and think—is it big?" • "Remember dad saying, 'You'll end up the size of a house'". • "Don't want anyone looking at me and thinking [what dad said]".	• Being aware of my body shape and weight. • Comparing body with cousins. • Thinking I'm fat. • Thinking I can't tell people things like this or they get worried, this has to be a secret.	• Comparing facial features to sisters "beauty". • Thinking about own appearance—"ugly ducking". • Feeling "awkward" at ballet.

Bianca	Erica	Sally
• Thinking 'if my own family makes comments, what does everyone else see?' • 'Three more bites and then you can leave [the table]'. • Comparing to cousins. • Thinking I need to shrink to feel that same love. • Thinking and monitoring "fixation" on stomach. • Food is monitored by family members. • Body-image comments from family.	• Comparing weight to mother's weight. • Following fitness brands and fitness influencers.	• Joining dad on runs. • Drinking dad's health juices. • Going vegetarian.

Fiona	Courtney	Katrina
• Looking at people on Instagram. • Look in the mirror. Hate myself. • Comparing to people online.	• Comparisons with extended family. • Neighbours sexualise women. • Neighbours obsessed with body-image.	• Refusing food. • Giving food to the dog. • Throwing lunch away at school. • Fighting with parents at dinner time. • Not touching food or eating food with hands. Having to wash hands after touching food. • Separating foods so they did not touch. • Serving self a small amount. • Avoiding going out for meals in community. • Didn't want people talking about my food. • Vegetarian.

Prior discourses shaping the eating disorder behaviours

A dominant societal force shaping eating disorder behaviours were *neo-liberal discourses* that promote personal responsibility for health, health as morality, thinness as goodness, and optimisation. The neoliberal discourses shaping these behaviours were present in their language when they used words like *good, bad, naughty, treat, control, discipline, health, fitness, better, winning, less than*. While there was one father in this sample who was the primary caregiver modelling eating disorder behaviours, it was the *female family members* that were most often observed body monitoring, dieting and exercising, as they too were living in an environment that fostered these values.

Patriarchal forces were present in shaping eating disorder behaviour, when women spoke about bodies that were small or slight as being more pretty, beautiful or graceful than other bodies. *Being feminine* meant taking up less space, being refined and controlled. Almost every one of the women had similar themes around being "*the good girl*", and eating and exercising was one way that they did the right thing and avoided criticism.

Sometimes the women could identify who they were performing these discourses for, like family or friend audiences, but when it was explored further they often could not make sense of why. Sometimes it was for others in general, and sometimes it appeared to be for themselves or for the eating disorder. These general or abstract audiences are indicative of societal forces. Adora was able to articulate that being a "good girl" was a way for her to mitigate the shame that her parents experienced within their community following her birth.

Table 14.2 gives some examples of the language accompanying body size and eating in the women's early life stories prior to their eating disorder, which had themes of morality, personal responsibility for health and discipline, group norms and being socially valuable.

Gabby is a case of how societal forces can be filtered through group forces to become something unique. In high school, Gabby's thinness meant success and artistry within ballet, and it provided opportunities through her teachers, who would give her performance roles. Gabby was not pursuing *mainstream* (societal) feminine beauty standards and made efforts to avoid the male gaze at times. Yet ballet itself was shaped by the same patriarchal and gendered contexts and promoted worse behaviours through this group.

The women learned early in life *that discourses had power* when their bodies were the subject of other people's comments. While some women mentioned *negative comments*, most of the women were shaped by *positive comments* and *compliments about their body*. They learned that their *bodies were a valuable resource* if they followed the discourses underlying people's compliments on their bodies such as "like a model" and "thin and beautiful".

Restrictions on the women's behaviour

While all the women were living in *intensely restrictive contexts*, these rose for different reasons. For example, Gabby had little idle time in her busy family home,

Table 14.2 Language accompanying body size and eating patterns in early life.

	Morality (goodness and beauty)	Personal responsibility for health and wellness, discipline	Group norms (fitting in and standing out)	Socially valuable
Adora	• "Having a big bum was like a major crime". • "A beautiful person is virtuous".	• Looking after yourself.	• "I don't want anyone looking at me . . . and thinking, 'Oh god, look at that'".	• Overweight = not worthy. • Thinner = more appealing, accepted, wanted, attention. • I liked getting those compliments.
Gabby	• Beautiful. • Perfection. • Gracefulness.	• Discipline. • Healthy eating, gotta eat your vegetables. • No control. • Pizza treats.	• People will get worried, so I have to keep this to myself. • Wanna wear brother's big shirts, then mum is like wear this instead.	
Diane	• Beautiful vs Ugly. • Naughty food.	• Food is a treat.	• I don't care what my peers think of me.	• Thinness = control.
Bianca	• Skinny and pretty.	• Counteracting not having time for exercise by restricting food intake.	• "Ours makes a different noise". • "Oh wow, that's a big person". • Needs to be 10kg smaller than boyfriend. • Does not want to be negatively perceived.	• Skinny = idolised and gets better gifts. • Shrink = feel same love.
Erica	• Overweight is a bad thing. • Tiny waist/stomach is good.	• Healthy. • Eat clean. • Body like a temple.	• Anxious about being perceived by others.	• Appearance is almost before anything else.

Sally	• Bad diet. • Vegetarian is the right thing to do. • Tall and thin = beautiful.	• Thin = exercise, diets, healthy, juice cleanses. • No wonder they are unhappy, you can tell by their diet.	• Vegetarian because my dad and sister were. • Taller = masculine • You should have seen them.	• Inadequate, need to lose weight. • Tall and thin like a model.
Fiona	• Fatness and ugliness.	• Wanted to have abs.	• Wanted to look like people on Instagram. • Hate myself.	• Being good enough.
Courtney	• Being fat is bad. • Taking laxatives is cleansing.	• Thinner = healthier and in control. • Thin and fit. • Even those that are not fit are put together.	• Going to the gym with the neighbours. • Sexualised by neighbours. • Fear of "looking like shit".	• He notices me. • Look like a model.
Katrina	• Vegetarian is an ethical choice. • Something fundamentally wrong with that girl, she has anorexia.	• Point of control. • Tiny = a child. • Tiny = need to eat more, it's good to put on weight. • Don't tell me what I need to do.	• You just want to be different, hard work. • You should be grateful; your mum has worked hard. • Don't bring attention to it, just feed her. • Anorexia is taboo.	• Cooking is boring. • She was amazing and I loved her—slight and tiny and petite.

and ballet was a niche context which became increasingly restrictive with her success. Sally lived in a foreign-speaking country with her alcoholic father and was limited to her international school where she was bullied. Katrina lived in a small country town where she was highly monitored by her parents and bullied by her peers.

What the women considered to be the beginning of their eating disorders were *exaggerations* or variations of already practised behaviours. The exaggerations of behaviour followed an accumulation of *restrictive life events* like a car accident, sexual assault, physical and verbal abuse, isolation, death of a partner, relocation, failure, parents' separation and increased opportunity pressure. The women had little chance to change or escape these bad situations, and the bad situations themselves restricted their behaviour even further through collateral effects. The ways that these events changed their social relationships after the event was as important.

When their eating disorders emerged, all the women were mainly limited to their contexts of home and school, and we can see some patterns across these contexts. Their reputations at school or with peers were significant contexts, and many experienced bullying and reduced influence in this context.

- Adora was not taught how to have conflict with people without ending her relationships, and so she was restricted in how she could communicate.
- Diane was home-schooled by her mother, so her family context and school context were conflated, with little other social opportunities.
- Gabby did what the teachers said to avoid getting in trouble. She "put stress on herself" to perform well, but adults and teachers were the audience not peers.
- Gabby had a niche context of ballet throughout her schooling, and here her performance was always being measured through competitions, exams and performances. The teachers were described as intense, that they would yell, and could be very scary for a child.
- Bianca's high school boyfriend protected her from being bullied, so when he sexually assaulted her, she did not tell anyone.
- Sally's school cohort had a bully culture, and Sally was often a victim of bullying even amongst friends. There were little opportunities for friends outside of the school.
- Courtney was bullied by her own friend group and avoided school, but her non-attendance created more stress at home with her parents. She then spent time with her neighbours where she needed to engage in eating disorder behaviours to maintain the relationship as they were her only escape.
- Katrina was bullied at school for upholding the expectations of her parents, and there were little opportunities for other friends as she went to a small area school, some friends distanced themselves to avoid being bullied themselves, and one good friend moved away.
- When Katrina was sexually assaulted, her friends did not believe her and defended the perpetrator who was well known and popular in the community because of sport.

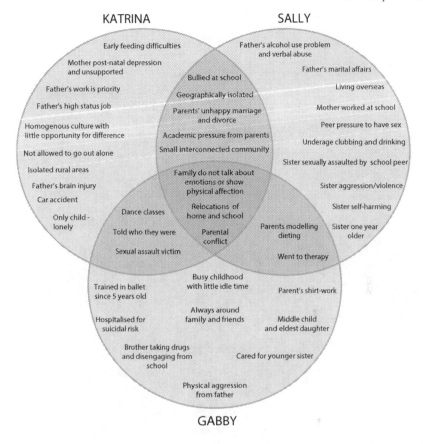

Figure 14.1 Diversity and overlap in three participants' specific life problems

In all this, we can see both common elements and elements unique to the individuals. Figures 14.1 and 14.2 give some indication of this with two groups of three women.

A common context shared by the women was their role in their family and accountability to their parents. As touched on in the previous section, the women played the role of the good girl especially in their immediate families. Being good meant giving their attention to others and not requiring much attention themselves, putting them in a position of lower power. The women's behaviour was restricted by their reputation in their family and how their parents would respond to their behaviour. They were often praised by their parents for being the good girl, and sometimes it was the only way that they could get attention or get their parents to do things for them. Getting attention by expressing or talking about emotions was often blocked by caregivers, who would dismiss or criticise these behaviours.

- Adora protected her mother from disappointment following her mother's suicide attempt.

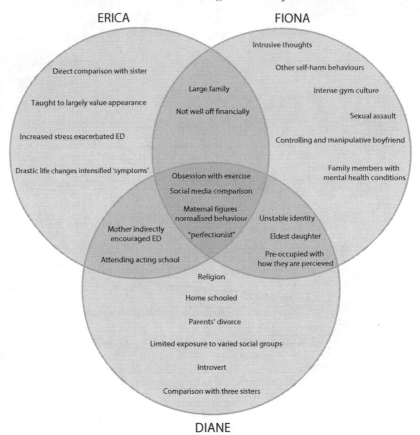

Figure 14.2 Diversity and overlap in three other participants' specific life problems

- Adora acted perfectly to prove to her community that her birth out of wed-lock was worth it for her parents.
- Gabby was the golden child in her family because of her achievements in school and ballet, and because she acted good (being quiet, polite, clean and still).
- Diane was aware of her parents' stress and said she was a very good child.
- Erica's reputation with her family was to be nice, well-behaved, a good student and a good daughter. Erica lived a busy schedule of school and extra-curricular activities including sports and theatre. The main audience of these achievements were her parents.
- Sally's father would get so drunk that he could not be a parent and they would have to look after him, while her mother was monitoring her school grades and the people that she spent time with. Fiona did not want to worry her parents because they already had so much going on, and it was her job to pick up the pieces and make everyone proud.

- Courtney's mother became unwell with depression and her father was often absent while he was studying. Courtney then took on the responsibility of her younger sister.
- Katrina was expected to be good; her emotions were wrong and inconvenient, such that her significant car crash injuries were swept under the rug.

The women were living within a nuclear family of a married cis-gendered couple, traditional gender roles shaped unhappy marriages, and marriage contracts kept them together long after they were working. The parents were reported to stay together 'for the children' even though there was little affection, and sometimes conflict.

- Adora's parents got married because they were pregnant with her, which was communicated to her across her life along with expectations, shaping the narrative that she needed to be perfect to prove that she was worth it.
- Gabby's family relocated in her early years for her father's work, which reduced extended family support compared to Gabby's sister. Gabby's mother was the primary caretaker of children and household duties, despite returning to work shortly after giving birth. Both parents were busy, and there was little structure at home.
- Gabby's relationship with her own mother was impacted by her grandfather who was abusive towards the family, leaving Gabby's grandmother to work and raise the children.
- Bianca's father was working 7am–7pm, then going to his parents' house to care for his father who was paraplegic and wanted to continue living at home. Bianca's mother gave "too much attention" to the siblings to "offset" his absence.
- Sally's parents relocated overseas for her father's work, where the family had no support from extended family. Her mother had little influence in the marriage, and she put up with an abusive husband to avoid split custody of the children.
- Courtney's parents used to "fight quite a bit . . . had that stupid notion that parents need to stay together for the kids . . . you're just harming the family more".
- Courtney's mother was the primary caretaker of children and household duties; when her mother was depressed, her father was absent doing his PhD, and Courtney was expected to take on more caring roles.
- Katrina's mother had little support from her father because babies were women's business, and his work was the priority. The family relocated so that her father could continue working in local politics, even though he was commuting back to their farm every weekend, and her mother had no connection in the new community. Her parents avoided divorce despite not loving each other and having conflict.

The division between private family life and public family life was also restrictive. The children did not know who to talk to or how to talk about the things that were going on at home without it damaging their reputations. The children's peer relations were restricted by the secret of their parents' neglect, drinking, alcoholism, fighting, verbal abuse and physical abuse. Realistically, it was easy to hide their bad family situations as most of it occurred inside the privacy of the home. But to avoid these details coming out in conversation, verbal tricks like lies or distractions are still required.

We are not *blaming* the parents, who themselves were raised in contexts that engendered their behaviours restricting their children. Sympathetically, the parents were also shaped by *capitalist forces* when they acted to provide their children with opportunities to attain education, employment and long-term income. In the context of a capitalist economy, being a good parent also meant encouraging hard work to achieve high standards and be competitive. The parents' socioeconomic status shaped the expectations they had for their children, because they wanted similar opportunities for their children, but also because their children's success could reflect on their own reputation. While parental pressure was concerned with the stability of income, the participants also experienced the pressures of contemporary capitalism, which additionally promotes social capital and the 'realisation' of one's 'passions' through work.

The overall picture from these nine stories is of diverse environments which are commonly restrictive and shape eating and body behaviours. This is summarised in Table 14.3.

What collateral effects did the unusual eating behaviours have on their life?

The women's environments only afforded salient opportunities that shaped eating disorder behaviour. Their eating disorders gave the women *influence* in their family relationships or allowed them to have an *effect* in their lives, or at least gave the appearance of these. Some of the direct and collateral (Guerin, 2022, "legacy behaviours") effects that eating disorder behaviours then had on their life included:

- Maintaining a *value* or *identity* that was assigned to them
- Fitting in, bonding or competing with peers
- Socio-economic opportunities: jobs as models, admission to ballet school, performance roles, jobs as fitness instructors
- Distraction and escape
- Something to do when there was nothing else to do
- Eliminating choices and decisions
- Rebuffing others
- Influencing others
- Getting help or being 'sick enough'
- Changing how they felt (like a sense of control, regulating emotions, anxiety, feel numb, adrenaline)

Table 14.3 Combined life issues of all nine case studies.

Stress	Restrictions	Eating and food	Discourses
Sexually assaulted.	Pressure from parents to be a good girl.	Parents fat-shaming women.	Overly harsh view of body.
Cousins favoured by auntie.	Shared room entire life with sisters.	Friends idolising thin women.	Fear of fatness.
Stress during COVID–19 pandemic.	Home-schooled entire life.	Being called "big-boned with small boobs".	Fear of being negatively perceived.
Unstable homelife (childhood).	Limited exposure to social peer groups.	Friends with ED.	Friends engaging in ED discourse.
Unstable homelife (young adulthood).	Not well off.	Body-image obsessed neighbours.	Body dysmorphia.
Increased stress. Drastic life changes.	Only child: no support or distractions.	Mother indirectly encouraged ED.	Fears of being negatively perceived.
Unstable self-identity.	Father's work is priority.	Obsessed with exercise.	Negative body-image discourse from partner's parents.
Controlling manipulative boyfriend.	Isolated in rural area.	Maternal figure normalised ED behaviours.	Direct comparison with sister from mother.
Religion.	Not allowed to go out.	Intense gym culture.	Taught to value appearance.
Parents' divorce.	Geographically isolated.	Early feeding difficulties.	Social media comparisons.
Family members with 'mental health' issue.	Small community.	Family history of eating disorder.	Perfectionist.
Serious car accident.	Mother worked at school.	Mother dieting and weight loss.	Unstable self-identity.
Father's car accident and personality change.	Reserved caring style from parents.	Ballet was escape but highly competitive, encouraged perfectionism and objectification.	Pre-occupied with how they appear.
Bullying at school.	Mother and daughter "dressing up" and going to events as accessories of father reputation and success.		Intrusive thoughts.
Academic pressure.	Boyfriend's family expects her to be quiet, polite, and look nice.		Constant comparisons with three sisters.
Father's alcohol problem.	Father's 'good girl' expectations are gendered. More restrictive because female (Father has greater trust in boyfriend.).		Told who they were.
Father's verbal and emotional abuse.			Journalism cadetship: competing with university students—'proving self', news cycle, workplace hierarchy, stories easily monitored by anyone and linked to reputation.
Father's marital affairs.			
Sister sexually assaulted by student.			
Sister's depression, self-harm and anger.			

(Continued)

Table 14.3 (Continued)

Stress	Restrictions	Eating and food	Discourses
Had diary read by peers. Peer pressure to have sex. Parental conflicts. School and home transitions. Parents working irregular hours. Physical aggression from father. Moved away from friends and grandparents to small country town where: —Bullied by peers —Small school —Did not fit into culture —High monitoring —Gossip Moved overseas away from mother's family where: —Small community —Bullied by peers —High monitoring Pressure to do well at school and go to university.	Middle child and eldest daughter expected to self-sacrifice. Older sister more dominant and aggressive. Older sister finishing school, moving away and leaving her alone. More independence leads to speaking up and abuse. No car, nowhere to go. Brother undisciplined, drinking and doing drugs. Busy childhood with little time for self. Rich students, lack of community and support. Job scarcity/security.		Parents worried about their reputation—daughter could not be known as 'the girl with an eating disorder' or mental health problems. She remains connected to town and gossip because of social media. Pressure to always be contact, keep up with everyone, and have it all, fear of missing out.

Much of the women's talk about emotions and feelings were omitted in this book because our focus was on context and observable events. But the women did often speak about their eating disorder behaviour to be influential on their feelings, or their experience of their feelings. But this idea of "emotion regulation" only explains the eating disorder if we subscribe to an 'essentialist' theory of emotions—that they are universal, hard-wired into us before birth, and triggered by events. However, a contextual theory of emotion offers a different understanding, that emotions do not originate from inside the person—that they are constructed from what is going on in the context, and created by the body preparing to act or have an effect in that context (Guerin, 2020). According to this theory, anxiety or stress could be when the context creates uncertainty around how to act, and the body mobilises excess energy to help someone improvise and learn what to do better next time. If learning does not occur, the anxiety may continue to arise in that context. Interestingly, this theory proposes that emotions have something to do with the power to act in a context and bring about expected effects.

So, in the case studies we find numerous outcomes of when eating disorder behaviours were useful to the life contexts of these nine women.

What life events led to some form of recovery?

Shaping of eating disorders was a two-part process: the restrictions on possible behaviours to deal with bad life contexts, and the shaping of eating and body behaviours to seemingly deal with bad life contexts. So, it makes sense that recovery was also a two-part process.

The first part was expanding their social opportunities or gaining greater influence in existing relationships, which was helped by finishing school, joining new study or work groups, and ultimately leaving their home situations. Leaving home was not always enough because parents continue to be an important audience. The women relied on their parents for resources after leaving home, the parents continued to monitor their behaviour, and the women described still having daughter obligations. The women had to find ways to achieve "relational distance" or gain more influence in the family. The women made mention of not being able to talk openly to their parents about the ways that their relationship impacted them, and this sometimes became easier with the less resource ties that they had, and with help from professional authorities like doctors. The women sometimes gained more influence by contextual changes that occurred for other members of the family, which changed the family dynamics and parental expectations, and opened new roles for the women.

The second part for recovery was finding new discursive groups where learning other ways of talking and acting around food and bodies was more effective. Achieving part two of recovery seemed easier for those women who had already achieved part one, but there were still many difficulties in ceasing their old behaviours:

- Their eating disorder behaviours were exaggerated normal behaviours, and many people around them practised the same or similar behaviours.

- Their caretakers were the ones who often modelled these behaviours, and one of the most consistent interpersonal contexts across most people's lives.
- Eating and your body are unavoidable, unlike something like drugs or gambling which occurs in a specific context.
- Work and study pathways were sometimes achieved through their eating disorder behaviour, so recovery required new study and work pathways.
- The societal discourses shaping their eating and body behaviours were always there, as we will see in the next section.

The role of language with eating behaviours

Keeping language secret was a theme for the women, which was not surprising since the eating disorder was a secret for the women most of the time. Sometimes language about eating and bodies was kept secret to avoid people knowing who might try and stop them—therapists, caregivers and partners. Some women used 'socially acceptable' language to restrict their eating around people who may try to stop them. Sometimes the women spoke more freely around others sharing their behaviour, but sometimes it was also secret around others known to share their behaviour, and maybe this was to do with competition as mentioned by Gabby and Sally.

Secrecy, and severe collateral effects of secrecy, occurred with all nine women, especially around bingeing, purging or compensating—behaviours that were further away from mainstream societal discourses shaping their eating disorder. Other times shame was experienced around people thinking they were materialistic, vain or hypocritical, and language was kept secret to avoid being stigmatised by others in a way that affected their reputations. For example, Adora had not vocalised her "fat-shaming" thoughts as she did not want to sound like her father, or make people feel the way her father made her feel.

The women had critical thoughts about their bodies and made efforts to change their bodies, but they did not want others to know this. Even in the women's stories about their caregivers, critical talk was spoken about as being saved for the privacy of their home. This seemed partially to do with creating an illusion that their body was innately *them* rather than the performance that it is. Image becomes disproportionately important in a society characterised by: few and brief exchanges upon which to build a reputation, technology that increases the divide between private and public reputation, and where competition and confidence are marketable qualities.

Women had reason to suspect that people have uncommunicated thoughts about their body, because of the vocalised and shaping discourses around being a good, kind or polite person. They also observed people in their life, often parents, talking negatively about other people's bodies when those subjects were not present. The secrecy of this language makes societal discourses less observable, which is one reason why it may seem that the thoughts themselves are causing the eating disorder. It also makes it more difficult for individuals to actively negotiate with the discourses and create group or cultural change. The women spoke of how challenging the talk of others was important to their own recovery, but if people are protecting the discourse by keeping the language secret even though they are following it in action and interpersonal exchange, little opportunity is provided for recovery discourses to influence others.

Thoughts or language about bodies and eating seemed to be the hardest thing for the women to change, often making them doubt if they were really recovered even if their actions did not reflect those thoughts. *Even when they had stopped overeating, under-eating and other actions, they still had anxious and intrusive thoughts about their weight, size and reputation.* Sometimes this was referred to as an 'eating disorder voice' but mostly after being in treatment, which may have something to do with the way that therapists contrast the 'eating disorder self' with the 'healthy self'.

For some women, the behaviour occurred without language attached. This was obvious in Katrina's story, where she avoided food at a young age with little reasons and only found language to describe fat-phobia after going through therapy. However, Katrina's refusal of food accompanied her secret language of rebellion "don't tell me what to do" (words that she did not voice). In the interview, Katrina described her refusal of food with pride, that there was nothing her parents could do to convince her to eat. She agreed there was a sense of power that came from saying no, but quickly followed with assurances that this behaviour was not intentional and more like "possession".

The women came to learn new ways of talking about themselves and their eating disorders, and this was an important part of recovery when it provided influence in relationships. The women often spoke about people's various "educations" in mental health, and how this impacted their ability to influence them with discourse they learnt through professional supports. The way that the women spoke about their eating disorders varied and was also shaped within their different contexts, including different types of interactions with professional supports:

- Adora's recovery was shaped by feminist discourses that helped to externalise the body-image discourse that was a driving factor in the development and maintenance of her eating disorder.
- Gabby developed a biomedical understanding of her eating disorder. Her treatment was based in the hospital where she was prescribed medication. The biomedical discourse helped Gabby ease her guilt around not being productive, which was likely shaped in the family as she described her mother to be busy and to "nag" her.
- Bianca began to imagine her eating disorder voice as Willem Defoe who she could then tell to "shut up".
- Sally sometimes referred to her eating disorder as a mental illness, but she was also able to identify the ways that her life events and relationships had shaped her behaviour. She also had experience in reading, writing and journalism, and read widely about mental health and eating disorders. Perhaps because she did not get diagnosed or treated for an eating disorder, and

instead spent time in therapy talking about her family and her father, she was able to understand her behaviour contextually.

- Katrina had a trauma–informed understanding of her eating disorder, which for her was both biological and relational. She was studying to be a trauma counsellor, and was diagnosed and treated in a specialist eating disorder clinic with a multidisciplinary treatment team. Her history in yoga and wellness culture also points to a more holistic lens. She also had experience with reading, writing and journalism, so she read widely on eating disorders, and this taught her about the good girl archetype.

The research on language and the behaviours of eating disorders needs more work, especially given the high incidence of the eating disorder voice. Some indications come through in the case studies. These stories indicate that the shaping of language and thinking was different to the shaping of the eating and exercise behaviours, and that one can occur without the other. This is interesting since changing language is sometimes the only intervention for eating disorder treatment, or the first thing they address before moving onto interpersonal issues, with societal issues rarely addressed.

Conclusions

It is not surprising that there are many loose ends. *Young women having more-than-usual restrictions put on their behaviour, in all cases by well-meaning parents, emerges as the main pattern in our research.* They have early histories of social and media influence through eating and body behaviours, and because of their specific major life restrictions, these behaviours then became grossly exaggerated. Upon leaving the restrictive family situations, the behaviours change, but the language behaviours (anxiety, rumination, intrusive thoughts) did not disappear until new *discursive* social groups were formed. Changing the contexts led to changing the unusual eating behaviours.

References

Guerin, B. (2020). *Turning psychology into social contextual analysis*. Routledge.

Guerin, B. (2022). *Reimagining therapy through Social Contextual Analyses: Finding new ways to support people in distress*. Routledge.

15 Summary 2

What shapes the unusual eating behaviours and what leads to recovery?

Referring back to Box 3.1 from Chapter 3, we can summarise our results along-side the Social Contextual model of how mental health behaviours get shaped in general. With the rich life stories from the nine women, we can now start to map out what shaped their eating disorders, even though there might be other variations for other women. We did not systematically pursue every step of the model in this research, and this would make for a good research or therapy project.

Summary results for basic contextual model of mental health

1. Bad life situations →

The bad life situations described by our nine women with eating disorders were not the same as for other mental health behaviours. When the eating disorders emerged, the women's behaviour was being controlled and restricted, commonly through parents' lifestyle, expectations and monitoring. This was done in hopes of raising children who had "good opportunities" and no trouble, but it reduced their agency inside and outside the home.

The women did not describe being a victim to ongoing physical abuse or bullying, overuse of punishment, or poverty inside the family, as is seen elsewhere for mental health behaviour. In general, the parents were mostly caring for their children's welfare, even by the girls' accounts.

2. These shape a lot of life responses →

The question is one of finding out how 'normal' girls resist parental control. Perhaps normal young women might talk to their parents and influence them to change, but our women described barriers to this strategy. The family often had a "just get on with it" attitude, which provided less discourse for talking. Many of the women describe their parents as being dismissive or critical when they did try to talk about serious things or express their emotions. The women could also

DOI: 10.4324/9781003453918-18

not get one parent to take their side for a variety of reasons such as: Parents made decisions together; parents were busy and absent; one parent was more passive and agreeable to avoid conflict. Extended families were not an option either because they lived far away, or they were an audience of their parents' behaviour and supported what was happening.

In the nine cases we saw many strategies to distract from or avoid parents' restrictions, but sometimes these activities strengthened the discourses that exacerbated the eating disorder—gyms, clubs, sporting and dance classes.

Physically resisting or exiting the situation was difficult for these young women. In contrast, young men would generally have less trouble physically resisting or exiting. Gabby described one of the few cases of being a woman amongst family violence and its complications, when she intervened in her parents' arguments and "talked back" to her father. During the same period she had evaded a sexual assault on the street, so while the violence was not "bad enough" to run away, the dangers of being a female who tries exiting without alternative accommodation are clear.

The occasional mention of the women keeping their home lives secret from others, such as teachers and friends, is worth researching further as it was not directly asked about in these interviews. One example of Katrina using verbal strategies to hide her parents' restrictions and put up with her bullying, was to say that she was more artistic and ambitious than her peers and she did not like the parties she could not attend.

3. These shape a lot of difficult and often damaging life patterns →

We did not ask the women directly about these other patterns. In other research, people with psychosis had many intermittent patterns including criminal activities and drug use, which were not successful in changing their bad situations. In our sample, distraction with drinking was mentioned by some. This was often done while continuing to meet their parents' expectations, required great secrecy to avoid their parents monitoring and was limited to weekends. Substance-use became more common once the women had left home, with Gabby and Sally describing how drugs exacerbated their eating disorders.

4. But under three special life contexts the mental health behaviours are shaped →

The parents of these nine women were by appearance, caring and loving and looking after them, making it difficult to perceive there being a problem. Many had few other examples to compare parental behaviours, and assumed theirs was normal and that their own problems were not due to parental control and over-monitoring. Had there been an abusive parent enforcing restrictions heavy-handedly, the source of their problems would have been more obvious.

So, for the people with behaviours of eating disorders, it is not clear where the bad events are coming from. The parents can be over-controlling but not only is it unclear why, it is often claimed to be for love and for their children's own good. In a more troubling case where there was an outwardly physically abusive father, it was still unclear what made him do this, why he chose the recipient or what it would take to stop it happening.

5. Then mental health behaviours are shaped →

The nine case studies show that the eating and body behaviours were learnt from a variety of sources: societal discourses and media, groups online, school, more immediate friends and family members.

The eating disorder behaviours were commonly modelled by parents, and since parents were the ones who were restricting their behaviours, this was something they could likely get away with. Eating disorder behaviours were in the scope of 'good' behaviour and allowed them to do all the things they had to do, get out of the house, socialise, work, study and be a good girl. The eating disorders rarely received bad attention and often received praise or compliments. By the time the women had finished school and could leave home, these behaviours were a solid part of their behavioural repertoire, and often helped maintain access to friendship groups or occupational opportunities.

Another point is that exaggerating eating and body behaviours generally requires little in the way of resources and other people. They were always provided with food so eating was a salient behaviour to manipulate. To be shaped into only distraction with drugs, for example, would require more social contacts, money and alibis, which many of the young women would have difficulty accessing or sustaining. Contrary to this point, Katrina was later spending hundreds of dollars on special health products that she used to restrict her diet. Some of the women also mention boyfriends and friends doing drugs, a context where access was less shaping.

6. Which behaviours occur depends on circumstances and which behaviours are possible →

The exaggerated behaviours of eating disorders were not directly related to parental overcontrol, so we should not overly interpret their actual forms. Could the girls have done other behaviours? Well, yes, they did. All through the case studies there were examples or hints at other exaggerated behaviours of anxiety (planning, worrying, pursuing perfect grades in academia), depression (withdrawing from school, not leaving the house, staying in bed) and risk-taking (self-harm, thoughts of suicide, drinking and sleeping with peers). These other behaviours came and went, but for these girls the eating behaviours became 'locked in'.

Their eating disorder behaviours were effective in different ways and mostly went unnoticed by people around them. The women mainly kept their eating disorder secret from their parents, and this was often attributed to not wanting to worry or burden them. Maybe the women anticipated their parents would become more controlling in an effort to help their daughters. Cases outside of this project are known in which the parents became obsessed with stopping the eating disorder as they were loving parents.

There are hints across the case studies, that the discourses around eating and bodies were shaped differently to the physical actions, as thoughts existed without actions, and actions sometimes existed without thoughts, but more needs to be found out about this.

We can also get some ideas about why these unusual eating behaviours mainly occur for younger, western women, and few males and not in Asia until recently. The younger women were the ones with restricted lives and with few alternative behaviours they could control. Typically, in the west (and elsewhere), boys have much more freedom to do other behaviours if their lives are being restricted, especially using physical actions, bullying and exiting to resist parents. They also have privileges under most patriarchies for greater freedom in their behaviours. Finally, some informal talks with Vietnamese girls seemed to indicate that they had little control over eating and food. They were required (shame on the family otherwise) to eat everything given to them. So, this might not be a behaviour they can control *at all*, so would not appear as a mental health behaviour when in a bad life situation otherwise. But more research is needed to verify this and other contextual events going on with other groups from around the world.

7. Changing these patterns (recovery)

The general pattern was that when the women got away from the restrictive life situations, the eating disorder behaviours changed, and eventually reduced or ceased alongside changes in social relationships. Redefining life disruptions occurred in diverse ways: moving interstate or overseas, moving in with a boyfriend, getting a job in another place, etc. But the pattern was clear: *change the bad life context and change the behaviour.*

The case studies suggest that language is shaped differently from other actions, and the *discourses continued regardless*: the 'fear' of fatness, the critical thoughts about their bodies, thoughts about avoiding food, etc. The women needed a strong shift in their regular discursive groups to challenge the eating disorder discourse that sometimes continues in thought. Some learnt from therapy to challenge eating disorder thoughts by externalising them and assigning them to another 'entity'. Some recoveries required avoiding certain groups, or actively challenging eating disorder discourse when faced with fat-phobia in their interpersonal relationships. Some learnt from therapy and books to challenge patriarchal discourse in the media (especially Adora), or capitalist discourse in the health and wellness industry (Katrina).

What shows through the women's stories is that recovery is not a cure. The medical model is incorrect to think that the 'mental health diseases' are cured and stopped (Chapter 2). The behaviours are possible again *if bad life situations were to occur again.* These interviews occurred during the COVID-19 pandemic, and all the women mentioned how the new restrictions were followed by an increase in their eating disorder thoughts and sometimes actions. All the women spoke about the behaviours being easy for them to take up again.

In Box 15.1, we summarise the eating disorders but lose the diversity of each step in real lives (cf. Box 3.1). There is overlap with other behaviours of mental health as well as other pathways such as bullying and criminality. But it shows starkly the main contexts in life that shape these pernicious behaviours.

Box 15.1 Basic contextual model of unusual eating behaviours

1. Bad life situations →
Strong oppression or life restrictions. Many possible alternative normal behaviours are blocked

2. These shape a lot of life responses →
Escape the bad life contexts (but rarely possible)
Exit the bad life contexts (at least eventually)
Distract themselves from the bad life contexts
'*Put up with*' the bad life contexts
Hide the bad life contexts so at least other people do not make it worse

3. These shape a lot of difficult and often damaging life patterns →
Putting up with it, hoping for a change

4. But under special life contexts →
✓ Responses which might be expected in normal circumstances to help change the bad situations are not possible
✓ Any alternative behaviours are blocked or restricted, usually by people or bureaucracies
✓ The sources of, or responsibility for, the bad life situations are not easy to observe

5. What are labelled as 'mental health' behaviours are shaped →
These are normal behaviours which become exaggerated or morphed when they have no effect to change things
The behaviours might be unrelated to the immediate situation so they will not make sense to casual observers
The behaviours become chronic if they get locked into the bad life situations
Language and non-language behaviours shaped in different ways

6. Which behaviours occur depends on circumstances and which behaviours are possible →
Behaviours which appear to give some control
Behaviours which are even possible given the life restrictions and oppressions
Behaviours already known by observation of others and media

Behaviours which have been modelled by others around or are salient
Behaviours which can be exaggerated and morphed if necessary
Behaviours requiring few resources

7. Changing these patterns
In general, changing the life situations changes (not stops) the behaviours
Language and non-language behaviours need different sorts of contextual
   changes in discursive communities
Bring the same life situations back and relapse occurs, such as during the
   COVID pandemic for some.

Benefits of this analysis

The basic summary can be repeated for all the behaviours labelled currently as
'mental health'. It provides a way to better understand the diversity and com-
plexities involved, as there are many different contexts that come into play to
shape any behaviour. This opens up so many new ways to explore, understand
and change these behaviours which hurt people, beyond trying to fix something
'inside' a person.

Something we did not do systematically in this research was explore the life of
the parents, carers and other people involved. Since most of the caregivers modelled the eating disorder behaviours and helped to construct the environments
in which the eating disorders were shaped, it would be helpful to know more.
Some of their stories indicate that their parents were dealing with their own
life restrictions regarding money, work, relocations and their own parents' and
community expectations; and that parents also showed mental health behaviours
like depression, anxiety, substance use, thoughts of suicide and suicide attempts.
Despite this stress they were loving and caring, but too caring. It would have
been fruitful to do further research to explore the life contexts of these parents
and carers—what happened in their lives that restricted what the girls could do?

This brings up an important point for contextual analysis. We must separate
understanding from placing *responsibility* or *blame*:

- *understanding* comes from mapping all the life contexts and how they ramify
  on each other and have collateral context effects
- *responsibility* comes from the rules of a group or society as to how to manage
  and punish some people for their actions, for the good of others

Contextual research does not directly deal with responsibility. We are not here
to make the parents and carers take blame for their daughters' behaviours, but to
understand how the contexts occurred. A larger study would include talking to
the parents and carers, which would give us a much better idea of the life conditions that shape mental health behaviours over generations.

Index

Printed in the United States
by Baker & Taylor Publisher Services